New Directions in

New Directions in Chenille

Nannette Holmberg

Credits

President . . . . Nancy J. Martin
CEO/Publisher . . . . Daniel J. Martin
Associate Publisher . . . . Jane Hamada
Editorial Director . . . . Mary V. Green
Design and Production Manager . . . . .Cheryl Stevenson
Technical Editor . . . . Laura M. Reinstatler
Copy Editors . . . . Tina Cook, Laurie Baker
Cover Designer . . . . Magrit Baurecht
Text Designer . . . . Stan Green
Illustrator . . . . Robin Strobel
Photographer . . . . Brent Kane

That Patchwork Place is an imprint of
Martingale & Company.

New Directions in Chenille

Martingale & Company
PO Box 118
Bothell, WA 98041-0118 USA
www.patchwork.com

Printed in China

05 04 03 02 01 00 6 5 4 3 2 1

Library of Congress Cataloging-in-Publication Data

Holmberg, Nannette
New directions in chenille / Nannette Holmberg.
p. cm.
ISBN 1-56477-275-6
1. Patchwork. 2. Novelty fabrics. 3. Tufted textiles.
4. Quilted goods. I. Title.
TT835.H556225 2000
746'.04—dc21 99-047728

Mission Statement

We are dedicated to providing quality products and service by working together to inspire creativity and to enrich the lives we touch.

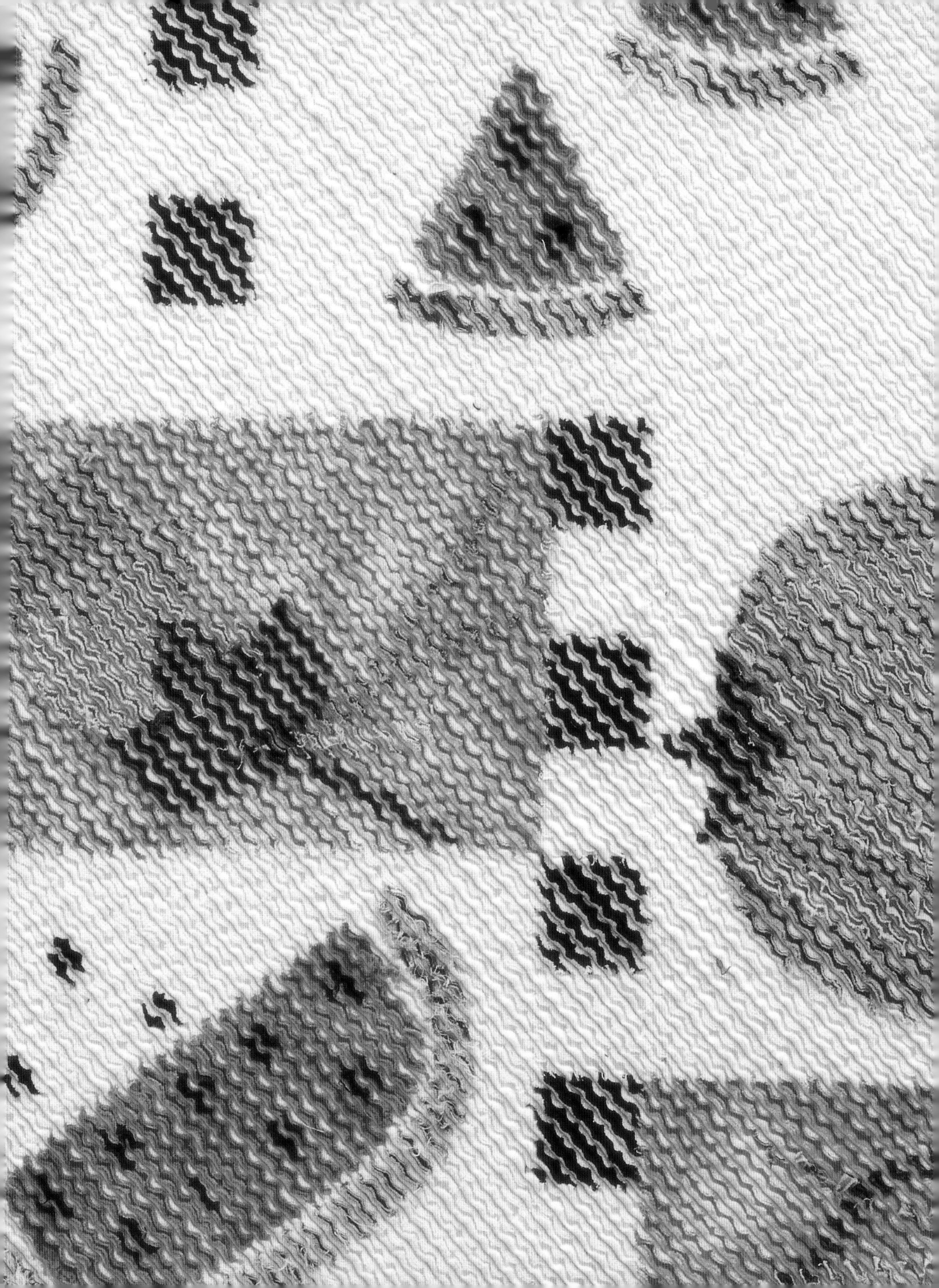

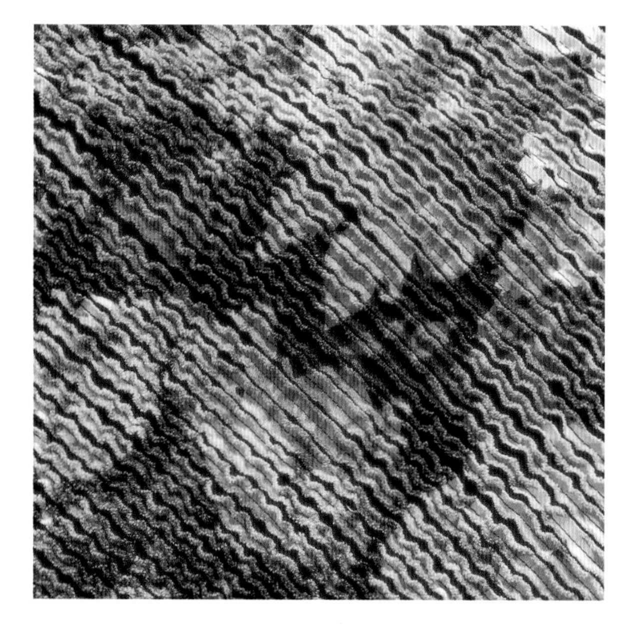

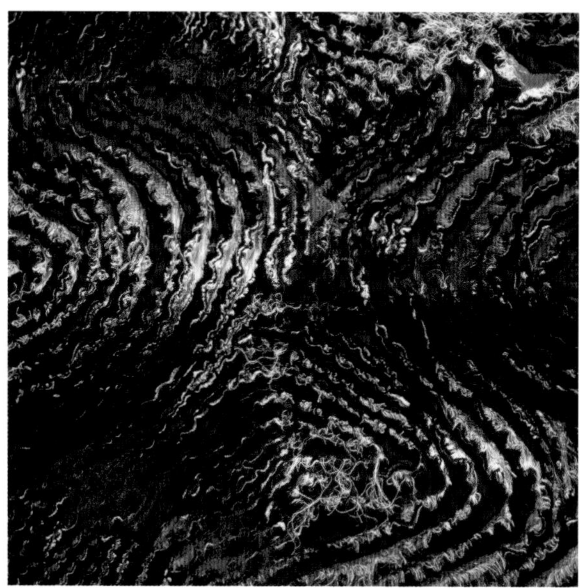

Contents

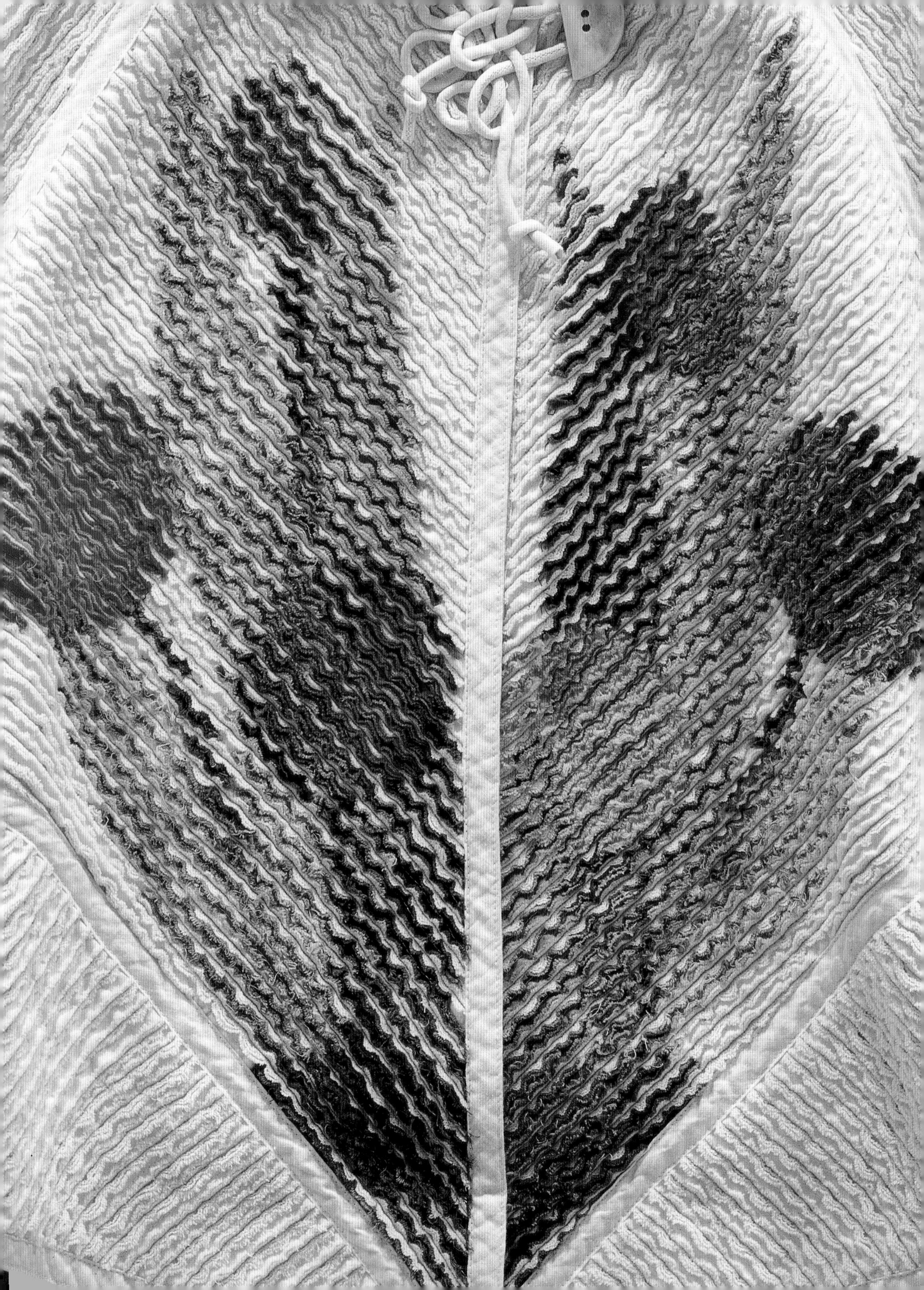

Introduction

The most difficult task in writing a second book about chenille was tearing myself away from my sewing machine long enough to write it. The longer I remained at the machine, the more possibilities evolved. The endless combinations of fabrics filled the floors of my studio. The rampant possibilities and variations became more and more exciting with the creation of each new sample block. Sketches covered tables and chairs and sat on top of fabric piles. Each sample block inspired a new design and application. Each design took on a different look as I varied the fabrics, the layering, and the channel widths. Discovery became infectious and I was on the brink of becoming addicted to what had already become a passion.

How did this passion for stacking and slashing layers of fabrics begin? It all started with a simple introduction to a technique called stitch-and-slash. Captivated by the process, I began to explore different fabrics. It was then that I discovered the wonderful qualities of rayon and the beautiful results I could achieve with it in the stitch-and-slash process. Rayon allowed me to use wide channels (½" to ⅝" between stitching rows) and it formed fluffier and fuller chenille than other fabrics I had used. Using rayon as a base layer also allowed me to design garments that had a soft drape and fluid movement, despite the many layers.

When I began making jackets and vests from the layers of soft, deep-pile fabrics I was creating, I searched for a name for this new fabric. Because it had the look and feel of old-fashioned chenille, but used rayon instead of the traditional cotton, I named the new fabric "Faux Chenille™."

My first book, *Variations in Chenille*, introduced the world to the process of stacking fabrics to yield a finished product with the look and feel of chenille. But while I was happy with the chenille "recipes" I had developed, I continued to explore the possibilities.

With the gift of a Japanese quilt book, I discovered a new perspective on the technique. Japanese quilters were doing new things with cotton that fascinated me. I was hooked again, as you will see in the chapters that follow. Let me take you on a journey into the "new directions in chenille."

What's New?

Cotton: The "New" Chenille Fabric

When I first tried using cotton to make chenille, I had limited success. Combinations of cotton fabrics proved interesting and often dramatic, but they never fluffed up as nicely as layers of 100 percent rayon fabrics.

In Japan, however, rayon is sold in limited quantities, so fiber artists there use readily available cotton fabrics to make chenille instead. With a few simple adjustments in the procedure—using fewer layers and stitching the quilting channels closer together—layers of most cotton fabrics bloom, or fluff up, successfully. The child's vest and bag on this page are examples of a Japanese cotton print layered with two coordinating cotton solids to create a totally new look in chenille. Because the rows of stitching are narrow (3/8" apart) and the fabric stack is limited to three layers, the fabric retains the images printed on the top fabric after washing. The lower layers of solid fabrics give lift and dimension to the images, which almost appear to have been painted on the surface, for a subtle, three-dimensional effect.

Child's Teddy Bear Vest and Bag by Nannette Holmberg, 1998; collection of Eva Schafer. Made of four layers of 100 percent cotton, this vest and bag feature a teddy bear print as the top layer. Vest made from an original design by Nannette Holmberg; bag adapted from a pattern by Laura Williams Dennison.

Successful results with cotton fabric are dependent on stitching widths and number of layers. The rows of stitching should be ¼" to ⅜" apart, and no more than four layers of fabric should be used. In contrast, when using rayons, the rows of stitching work best ⅝" apart, with five or six layers of fabric.

The vests shown on this page, made from the same pattern, illustrate the difference that fabrics and stitching widths make. On the left, all-rayon layers and wide stitching channels form a deep, plush pile. The vest on the right, made with both rayon and cotton fabrics and stitched with narrow channels, has the look and feel of wide-wale corduroy.

I have always stressed the importance of stitching the channels at a 45° angle to the straight of grain. But I have found it even more critical when working with cottons. Stitching at this angle will create the softest, richest, most consistent chenille, and the fabric will fray and fluff evenly on both sides of the stitching. To achieve the best results, pay close attention to the direction of the grain lines—doing so makes a great deal of difference. Cotton has little desire to fluff up and create a pleasing texture unless the stitching and cutting is done on the true bias (45° angle).

Two Vests by Nannette Holmberg, 1998. The vest on the left is made of six layers of 100% rayons and stitched in ⅝"-wide rows. The vest on the right includes four layers of both cotton and rayon fabrics and was stitched in ⅜"-wide rows. Both vests are made from McCall's pattern 2436.

"What's black, white, and red all over?"
Detail of jacket by June Colburn, 1996. Curved stitching over layers of silk creates an uneven texture accented by loose threads.

The closer the stitching angle approaches the straight of grain (either lengthwise or crosswise), the more shredding or stringing you get. An irregular stitching pattern, like the one shown opposite, produces floppy chenille, making it necessary to give the fabric a "haircut" so that it will look presentable.

You will also achieve better results if you select cottons that are yarn dyed. A yarn-dyed cotton is not printed with color but woven with yarns that have been dyed to the desired colors. This type of fabric will make a deep, clear coloration that you cannot achieve with most printed cottons.

Yarn-dyed fabrics work especially well when you want to achieve a clear and distinct image or shape. As we do more with the chenille layers in the following sections in the book, we will find additional ways of using these rich fabrics.

Further experimentation with cotton fabrics led me to several surprising finds. While these fabrics aren't new to sewers, they are new and wonderful additions to the chenille process that I hope you will try.

Muslin

One fabric that has been a continued source for me in creating this new cotton chenille is muslin. I find myself using endless amounts of it, both bleached and unbleached. When muslin is layered it becomes the perfect chenille canvas. It's great for the lower layers of a chenille stack, allowing you to use fewer more-expensive cotton and rayon layers. When you want to do a large project, such as a quilt, you will find that using muslin for the chenille layers produces a wonderful soft texture (see "Erin's Quilt" on page 25).

The Captain in Chenille by Nannette Holmberg, 1998. Four layers of yarn-dyed cottons create a rich look. This jacket was commissioned by Mission Valley Textiles and made from a pattern in Nannette's first book, *Variations in Chenille*.

Pre-Quilted Muslin

Pre-quilted muslin offers wonderful possibilities for chenille projects. It is composed of a base layer of muslin, one or two layers of cotton batting in the middle, and another layer of muslin on top. The fabric is available with various stitch patterns, but the one that works best for chenille has a 45° zigzag design quilted in ¾"-wide channels. Since a 45° angle is perfect for chenille, this zigzag-quilted muslin makes a terrific convenience product.

The three-layer muslin (with a single layer of batting) is perfect for pillows and projects requiring a lighter, more drapable weight, such as jackets or vests. For home-decorating projects like rugs and pillows, the four-layer quilted muslin (with the double layer of batting) will provide more depth and weight.

The sample block shown at right is an example of chenille made with the four-layer, pre-quilted fabric. A printed cotton fabric was added to the top and then the layered fabrics were re-stitched from the back over the original lines of stitching. The top half of the sample was cut after stitching over the original ¾"-wide rows of stitching. On the lower half of the sample block I first stitched over the original stitching, then stitched between the rows. This created narrow rows of stitching to make the new narrow-wale look. There is a clear difference in the effect between the widths of the channels.

If you wish to see more of the surface fabric, you need to make the distance between your rows of stitching smaller. The narrower the rows, the more you will see the pattern or colors of your top layer of fabric. This is especially important if you are using a print and you want to be able to see the design after the chenille has been washed and dried.

It is also easier to achieve the intricate herringbone design in a project using pre-quilted muslin because you have a pattern to follow when you stitch your rows. It is much easier to stitch an even, precise pattern while keeping accurate grain lines as well. Anyone who has made a chenille project with a herringbone pattern will know how difficult it is to stitch a large area with continuous pivoting, while trying to maintain even rows without losing the 45° angles.

Another attribute of pre-quilted muslin is its ability to be dyed. The muslin and the needlepunched cotton batting both accept dye readily (see "Dyeing Fabrics" on pages 20–21).

Flannel

Another fabric in the cotton family that is fun to work with is cotton flannel. Not all cotton flannels are successful—sometimes the weave just isn't right, or a finish might have been applied that inhibits blooming—but when they work, they are wonderful.

I especially like to use flannels in projects for children, although flannels are great fun in a warm fall jacket or vest for an adult. The wall hanging and matching teddy bear shown below are both layered with 100 percent cotton flannels for a child's room. And cotton flannels are perfect for a cuddly soft baby's blanket or throw.

Chenille Wall Hanging and Bear by Nannette Holmberg, 1999. Made from six layers of 100 percent cotton flannel, this bear is especially soft and cuddly. The bear coordinates with the wall hanging, also made from layers of cotton flannel. Simple designs and the child's name personalize the quilt. The teddy bear is McCall's pattern 9619.

New Ingredients and Techniques

With the discovery of what happens to cottons when we decrease the layers in a fabric stack and narrow the stitching rows, we open up a new world of possibilities. These new ingredients added to your chenille recipe should give you ideas that *I* haven't thought of yet! Begin to explore and experiment with your fabrics. You'll be amazed at what works, and better yet, you'll be impressed with your fabulous results.

Confetti Chenille

Why limit yourself to yardage off the bolt? Let's begin by throwing a few things into the mix that are foreign to the usual chenille process. Everyone has scraps. They may be scraps of fabric, snippets of ribbon, or odd pieces of yarn. You might wish to select just one type of scrap or you may want to throw everything in at once! This is a true free-for-all and will become what I like to call "confetti chenille." This method can be used with all types of fabrics and all kinds of fabric stacks, whether you're working with wide rows and many layers or narrow rows and just a few layers.

We'll use the vest shown below to illustrate the process. Start with four layers—the base and three layers of black rayon.

Confetti Vest by Nannette Holmberg, 1999. Scraps of hand-dyed silk ribbons and silk threads add color and texture to the chenille.

First, place two of the rayon layers on top of the base layer as shown below. Spray the surface lightly with temporary spray adhesive to help hold the scraps in place.

Do not put any pins in place at this time. Now, begin to randomly place—or throw—scraps of fabric, small pieces of ribbon, or strands of yarn over the surface. With your fingers, press the scraps in place to make sure they're caught by the adhesive.

The number of pieces you include on this layer will determine how much confetti will show in the final process. If you want a lot of color or texture to show, then add scraps until the second layer is completely covered. If you wish to have only areas of color or additional texture, place stacks of scraps in desired spots. This will give you splashes of color and texture.

After you have added the scraps, place the third layer of fabric on top of the stack. Place pins around the edges and fairly close together over the top layer to help secure the loose pieces you sandwiched between the layers. Pin frequently—you don't want the pieces to shift while you're stitching. Now you can draw the grain and stitching lines and quilt the layers.

Large Scraps

Placing large scraps and shapes on top of the second layer can give you interesting areas of color. If you do this, however, try to keep the grain lines of the larger pieces aligned with the grain lines of the cut layers so that you get areas of color only and not areas of raveled threads. Although you can give your final piece a "haircut," it will not have as much color as it would if you had aligned the grain lines. When you trim all those unwanted threads away you are cutting away much of the color and some of the fullness. Haircuts work, but your finished chenille is not the same as it would have been with proper grain lines. After several wearings and after each laundering, further hair trims may be necessary. Unless you are doing it for a special effect, avoid unaligned grain-line combinations.

Ribbons and Trims

Along with your aging fabric stacks you probably have shelves of aging trims and ribbons. The ribbon shown at right had, by itself, little chance of ever being applied to one of my wearable art pieces. The colors were reminiscent of a three-year-old's party dress and were somewhat dated. It was perfect for "R and D" (research and development). I began by placing the ribbon in rows on top of a cotton fabric stack. I stitched, slashed, and washed my sample. The result wasn't bad. The process made the ribbon look like part of the original fabric.

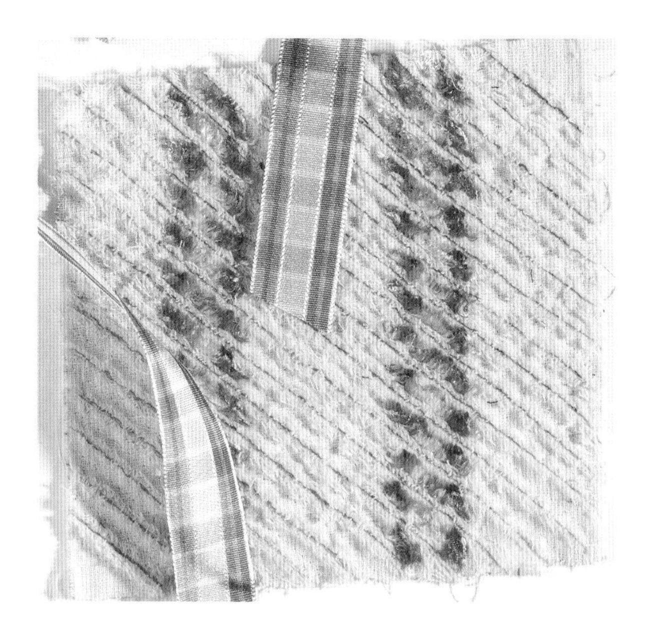

Realizing that the ribbon did have possibilities, I began playing with fabric and color combinations. My final fabric stack was a combination of cotton, rayon, and Qiana nylon. I stand behind my pledge to use everything in my basement eventually! The best part of the whole process was realizing I could fasten the ribbons to the top layer by using a gluestick. This held the ribbons flat and in place while I completed my rows of narrow stitching. (See the section on gluesticks and spray adhesive on page 29 of "New Tools and Products.")

I used ribbon-patterned chenille to make the bomber jacket shown below. But I didn't stop with simple plaid designs. I experimented some more and discovered that ribbons are

Bomber Jacket by Nannette Holmberg, 1999. This original design uses vintage rayon ribbon (shown above) to create a subtle plaid design over four layers of cotton and rayon fabrics.

also ideal for framing appliqués. In the jacket shown below, the leaf shapes were cut from a cotton ombré that had the same coloration as the silk taffeta ribbon. I used two shades of ribbon and two fabric colorations in the design. I cut some of the leaves on the grain line and some on the bias, allowing me to place them at different angles and still have an even chenille. (Remember to think of the grain-line placement when cutting your appliqué shapes.)

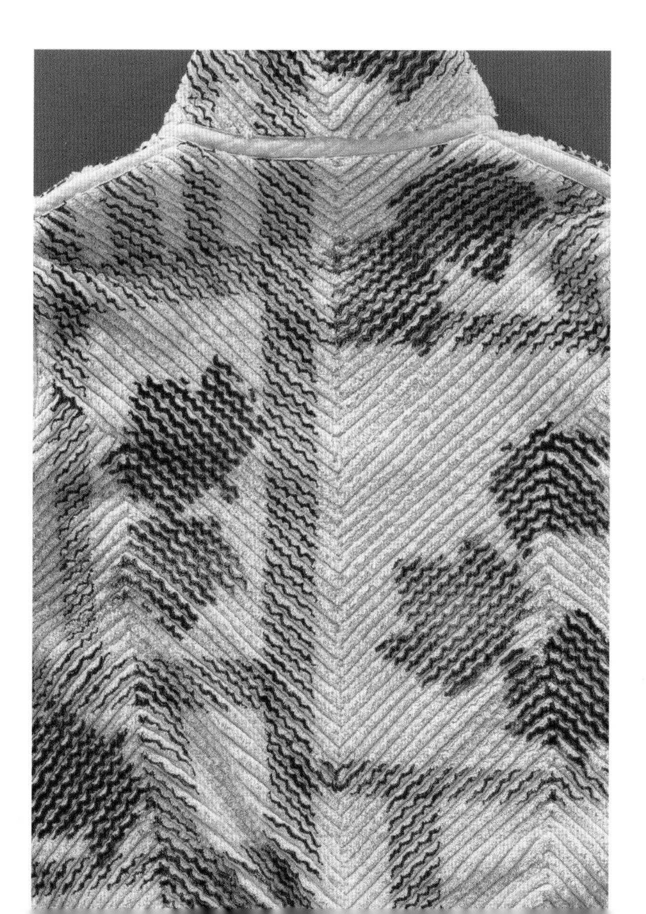

I used a gluestick to temporarily hold the appliqués and ribbon in place. A gluestick or adhesive spray is a big improvement on lots and lots of pins, which have a tendency to fall out or poke the unwary.

Appliqué on Chenille

The beauty of chenille appliqué work is that it does not require the raw-edge finishing that is necessary for traditional appliqués. There is no need to turn raw edges tediously around freezer paper or do heavy machine satin stitching. There are a few things you'll want to remember, however, so that the appliqués maintain definition.

When placing appliqué shapes inside a ribbon or fabric-strip framework, try to keep the images completely separate. It may look nice to overlap some of your leaves onto the ribbons, but you will find that even though the shapes stand out distinctly as you apply them, they will blend into the ribbon and lose their definition after washing.

It is important to remember what will happen to your appliqué in the chenille process. The rows of stitching should be ¼" to ⅜" apart on most cottons; wider chenille will distort the design on the top layer. After stitching, you will slash the layers and cut up your design.

Small, intricate designs are not good choices for chenille appliqué. Keep your designs bold and uncomplicated. Pictures from children's coloring books are good examples. Simple shapes, such as leaves, hearts, and basic geometric shapes are perfect choices to begin with. The appliqués blend into the stack just like ribbons do, becoming part of the final fabric—making it appear as though your top fabric layer has a design printed right on it.

The colors of the appliqués will seem to diminish and fade during the chenille process. This happens because the lower layers fluff and come to the surface after laundering, to become part of the appliqué coloration. So, select appliqués that are in high contrast to the base. If you want a lot of color in your appliqué design, select fabrics for your appliqués that are twice the intensity you want your final color to be. You can see the color change when you compare the sample block of the ribbon and leaf design on page 17 to the final project.

Strip Weaving

Another wonderful technique, especially for home decorating and wearables, is strip weaving. You will find directions for this technique and examples on pages 42–49 and 84–89 in the project section of this book.

Weaving creates surface designs with rich depth and exciting texture. Experiment with pattern, and don't limit your weaving to straight strips. For variety, cut the weaving strips in a wavy pattern as shown below. Just be sure to weave them together in the same order they were cut.

Uneven weaving sample from a vest by Nannette Holmberg. A yarn-dyed ombré cotton and a muslin square were cut into uneven strips, and then woven together in the order in which the strips were cut. The woven layer tops a muslin stack to create the unusual chenille design.

Kaleidoscope by Nannette Holmberg, 1999. Hand-dyed silk ribbons were woven over layers of black rayon to create a magical effect. Woven ribbons were added to the rolled side of the collar and cuffs, restitched on the original chenille lines, and left unslashed to add contrast and color to the finished coat. (Woven ribbon piece, right, by Peggy Neely.)

Dyeing Fabrics

For those who love to create their own colors with dyes and paints, this is an opportunity to explore new vistas. The fabrics that make the best chenille are natural fabrics. These are also the best fabrics to use when working with most dyes. I prefer fiber-reactive dyes, but even common household dyes can be used successfully in chenille projects.

One of my favorite additions to a stack of rayons or cottons is dyed, needlepunched cotton batting. The batting is absorbent and soaks up dye like a sponge. I like to put dyed batting just above the base layer and under the cut layers in the stack. The batting becomes one of the cut layers and adds softness and loft to the finished chenille. If you use a white batting, the colors will be deep and clear.

The process of dyeing the batting is simple. Household dyes will work well if you are unfamiliar with more professional fiber-reactive dyes. If you work with liquid dyes it will be easier to achieve even colors in the dye bath.

Dilute the dyes according to the directions and place the batting in the container until it has completely absorbed the color. Take the batting out of the dye bath and gently wring out as much of the liquid as possible. If the dye requires an additional bath to set the color, set the dye with the same immersion process, manipulating the batting as little as possible. *Do not put the batting in a dryer to dry. If you do, the batting will shred and fall apart.* Find a

Nannette's Signature Jacket by Nannette Holmberg, 1999. Various stacks of bright rayons were used in each section of this jacket. Needlepunched cotton batting, dyed bright yellow, forms the bottom layer of each stack to add additional color and texture to the plush chenille.

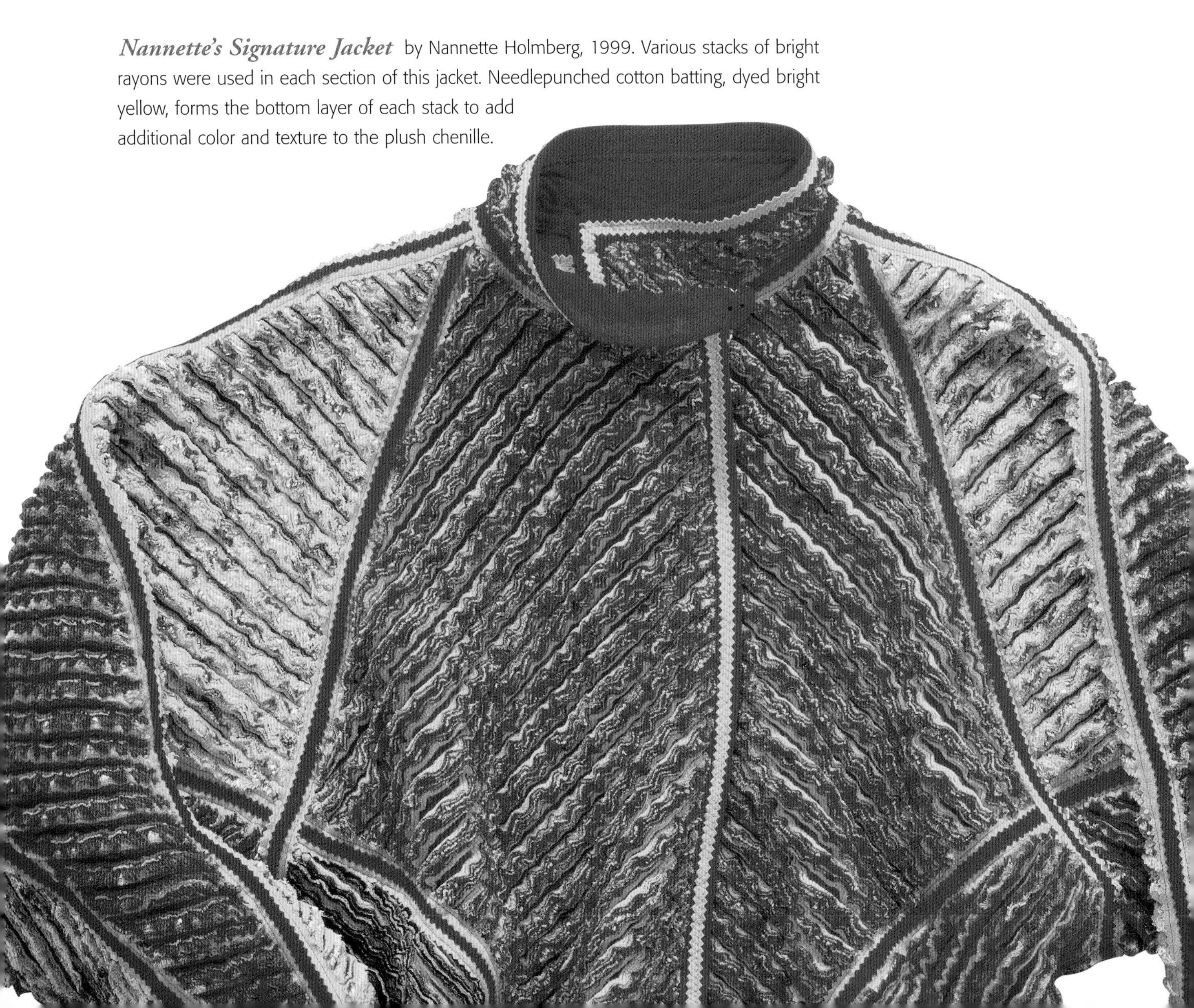

place to hang the batting where it can air dry. Once dry, it is ready to be cut and used like the other fabrics in your cut layers.

The jacket shown on page 20 has a layer of needlepunched cotton batting that I dyed bright yellow. For the remainder of the cut layers I used 100 percent rayons in bright prints and solids. I prefer to use rayons with my dyed batting because it keeps the finished piece soft and lightweight. Cottons can be used, but remember to use fewer layers and narrower rows for your wearables.

Pre-quilted muslin also takes dye beautifully (see the section on pre-quilted muslin on page 12). I've had the best results with fiber-reactive dyes. They seem to penetrate the layers of muslin and batting better than household dyes. I've also found it helps to make sure the fabric is completely wet all the way through before immersing it in the dye bath. Placing the dyed fabric in a tightly closed plastic bag for at least twenty-four hours will set fiber-reactive dyes.

For the jacket shown below, I dyed the pre-quilted muslin and batting a rich teal. To add texture, some sections were quilted only along the original ¾"-wide lines while others were stitched between the original lines as well. For further interest, I left some channels uncut and then stamped them with gold metallic paint.

Teal Jacket by Nannette Holmberg, 1999. Made with pre-quilted muslin, this jacket was completely constructed before being dyed and stamped with gold paint. The jacket is McCall's pattern 2436.

New Looks for Chenille

Wearables, Animals, and Accessories

By using narrower channels in the chenille process, we can now design garments with more structure and more detail. As few as three layers of any fabric combination in the cut stack will make a jacket or vest lighter in weight and less bulky. Designing wearables for chenille is similar to designing for a thick, plush fabric such as corduroy.

In addition to designing the lines and fit of the garment, you can also design the surface of the fabric. One of the most exciting possibilities is being able to place the design work exactly where you want it to appear on the garment. It is easy to match plaids because you can place the lines of the plaids where you need them to match at the side and shoulder seams of the garment. Uneven plaids are just as easy to match. Border designs around the bottom of a coat can be placed to continue perfectly past the side seams around the hemline without interruption.

The waistcoat jacket shown below is a perfect style for placing designs on the center front and back panels.

Muslin was my first fabric choice for this design because I wanted the flower appliqués to be the dominant theme of the garment. I used three layers of muslin for the stack that I would cut. Next, I marked off the areas for my floral design. Remember that appliqués should be simple. Keep your flower shapes bold—small shaded areas might be effective in normal appliqué designs, but they disappear in a finished chenille project. Remember also that

Tulip Waistcoat Jacket by Nannette Holmberg, 1999. Floral appliqués on layered muslin give this jacket the vibrant look of spring. The jacket is McCall's pattern 2162.

appliqués should contrast sharply with their background. I used bright colors for my floral jacket. If I had selected pastels or lighter colors for my appliqués, they would have faded so much after the garment was slashed and washed that I might have completely lost the design.

While I often cut the base layer slightly larger than the pattern pieces, you will have the best success if you cut your stacked layers to the exact size of the pattern pieces. This way the placement of your design will be accurate and you can match fronts, backs, and sleeves perfectly during garment construction.

I like to construct my garments completely before washing. This means I do all detail work, such as bias trims and seam finishing, before washing and drying.

In addition to using contrasting fabrics for appliqués, you can also use strips of fabric to create designs. The cotton vest shown on this page features both appliqués and a woven strip design.

The fabric strips for this garment were cut on the bias so they could be placed in a lattice-like design. Using a combination of strips and appliqués gives the vest more interest than if I had just used one or the other.

It seems only natural to use the chenille technique for children's projects. If ever there was a need for a soft and cuddly fabric that is washable, this is it! Children love the feel of chenille and can do no damage to it. Spill whatever you like on it—even the messiest ice cream cone will wash right out.

The child's jacket shown below has chenille in the main body, with machine-quilted sleeves. Small projects like this take very little fabric and can often be made from the scraps of larger projects. This jacket is made with small leftover pieces of rayons teamed with a denim-like fabric for the sleeves and trim. You can even use small leftovers for the non-chenille areas. Because I used rayons in the cutting stack, I was able to use wide stitching rows

Fabric Appliqué Vest (above) by Nannette Holmberg, 1999. Repeated layers of cotton in a tiny check make a great background for contrasting appliqué designs. The vest is McCall's pattern 8866.

Toddler's Hooded Jacket (right) by Nannette Holmberg, 1999.

to create a deep, soft chenille, and it took very little actual sewing time to create it.

Children's garments can be a great opportunity to experiment with cottons and use appliqué techniques to add the child's favorite animal (or even initials). The use of cotton prints is an easy way to bring their favorite characters to life.

You don't have to limit your chenille to clothing when designing for children. The bunny on page 105 was made with the same chenille process I use for my Faux Chenille jackets. Six layers of 100 percent rayons or cottons make up the chenille layers. The finished project is not only cuddly, he is—you guessed it—machine washable!

Grown-ups love chenille animals, too. You can make them either in off-the-wall designer colors or you can develop a coloration to match a bedroom or den. Creating the coloration is half the fun.

If you would like to do a fast project just to try the chenille technique before you dive into something serious, why not play with the idea of accessories? A handbag is a good starting point for a test run. There are wonderful patterns available for all types and sizes of handbags and totes. Begin with a simple design that has minimal detailing for a quick project (see "Watermelon Handbag" on pages 71–75).

Chenille bags present another opportunity to get into your scrap collection. It's your chance to play with the technique without getting into a major expense. (And you can clean out the floor of your fabric closet at the same time!) While you're in there, look for good pieces for appliqués or for the confetti technique.

Home Decor

Using chenille for home decorating is a natural; it's a wonderful place to play with texture and color. You can use chenille in every room of your house. Whether it's a luxurious rayon throw or a cushiony rug, you'll find chenille to be decorative as well as practical. Any time you have rugs and pillows that can be thrown in the washer when they're soiled is a practical plus.

Traditional chenille has become very popular again in the past few years. You see it in everything from bathrobes to decor for children's rooms. But the process of making old-fashioned chenille allows only one color in the tufted design area. You will see a lot of pastels and a few designs that include areas of different colors, but the process is limited. There is, however, no limit to the coloration you can develop when creating your own chenille for your home.

Peacock Pillow by Melanie Walker, 1999.

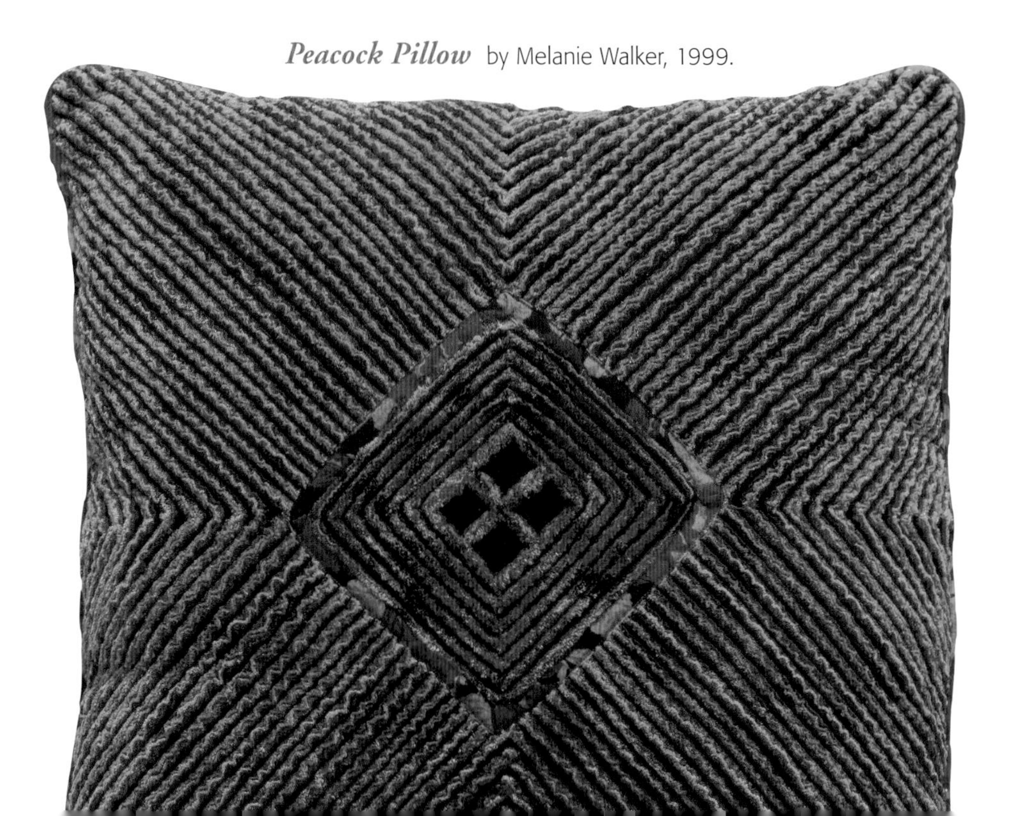

The fabrics used in home decorating are excellent to work with in the stacking layers. Even heavy decorator fabrics produce elegant texture when combined with muslin and needlepunched batting.

Pillows are a good place to start because of their size and simple shapes. By working with a square or rectangle of fabric, you can layer and make a pillow or pillow cover very quickly. They also offer a wonderful opportunity to sample some of the new techniques in this book. Try using appliqué, ribbon, or dyeing techniques for your pillow collection.

As you progress, move on to larger home-decorating items like quilts. The world of wearables and quilting go hand in hand. Some of the world's best quilters use their talents and techniques to create incredible wearable art. It seems only natural to take the transforming technique of chenille into the world of quilting.

I made the Basket block shown below using the appliquéd-chenille process. My new favorite fabric—cotton muslin—formed the base of my design. Muslin seems to be the perfect canvas for all types of traditional motifs.

Next, I put the process to the test by constructing a full-size quilt. I designed "Erin's Quilt," shown below, for my daughter Erin's wedding. I wanted to combine the Victorian look with Erin's love of flowers. The spray of tulips in the center of the quilt are framed with a large oval that I backed with pale blue. I created an outer frame of pink for the border. The finished quilt has a soft, watercolor effect, although the actual colors I used were very bright and intense. Simple diagonal stitching channels allow the appliqué design to show through.

Erin's Quilt by Nannette Holmberg, 1998. After going through the chenille process, vibrant floral appliqués soften into an elegant Victorian design.

When I make a chenille quilt, I start stitching in the middle of the quilt to stabilize the stacked layers, rolling one end and pinning it out of my way while I work at the machine. I stitch the ⅜"-wide rows until one-half of the quilt is complete. Then I roll and pin the first half and stitch the second half of the quilt in the same manner.

I slash the quilt with my rotary cutter and Omnistrips, page 28, being careful to advance the strips across the surface of the quilt as I cut to prevent the cutter from rolling over the end of the strip. Working with narrow rows makes it extremely difficult to slash with scissors because the channels are so restrictive. Using the strips and rotary cutter drastically reduces the time necessary to slash the quilt.

Once the quilt is completely stitched and slashed, I square up the ends and sides by using a long, clear plastic ruler and rotary cutter. Once I am sure the corners are perfectly cut at the proper angles, I bind and finish the quilt's edges.

The final step is to put the quilt in the washing machine with cold-water detergent to remove the adhesive residue. Then I dry the quilt in the dryer until it is completely dry.

Try using your favorite quilt pattern for a chenille quilt. The best patterns to use are simple shapes without detail. Designs with spacing or plain alternate blocks will set off contrasting fabrics.

I chose basic square and triangle shapes in the sample shown at right, placing black, red, and beige rayon fabrics on a stack of black 100 percent rayon. Because of the glue-stick-appliqué technique used for placing the designs, you can now begin to use fabrics that you have never used for quilting projects in the past. I know—you are a devout quilter who would never even consider using anything but 100 percent cotton for a quilt! Take a second look at the unique texture of this rayon quilt sample. It has a supple quality that one simply cannot achieve with cottons.

I loved the look and the feel of the rayon quilt block. Because it has an uncut base of rayon, cotton batting, and another layer of rayon in addition to the chenille layers, I was able to produce the weight and feel of a traditional quilt with the plush texture of rayon.

The "Cabin Fever" quilt (shown at lower right, opposite) is made entirely from rayons. It has a quilt base and three cut layers plus the quilting design work. I laid out all of the designs with temporary adhesive and stitched with ⅜"-wide channels. Simple quilt blocks combined with appliqués produced a beautiful, soft quilt to hang in a den or even spread on the floor. I knew after finishing this second quilt that the possibilities for quilts and wall hangings were going to be as endless as the designs that fill my notebooks for wearables. Try a few sample blocks, then make a couple of small quilts, and I think you will feel the same.

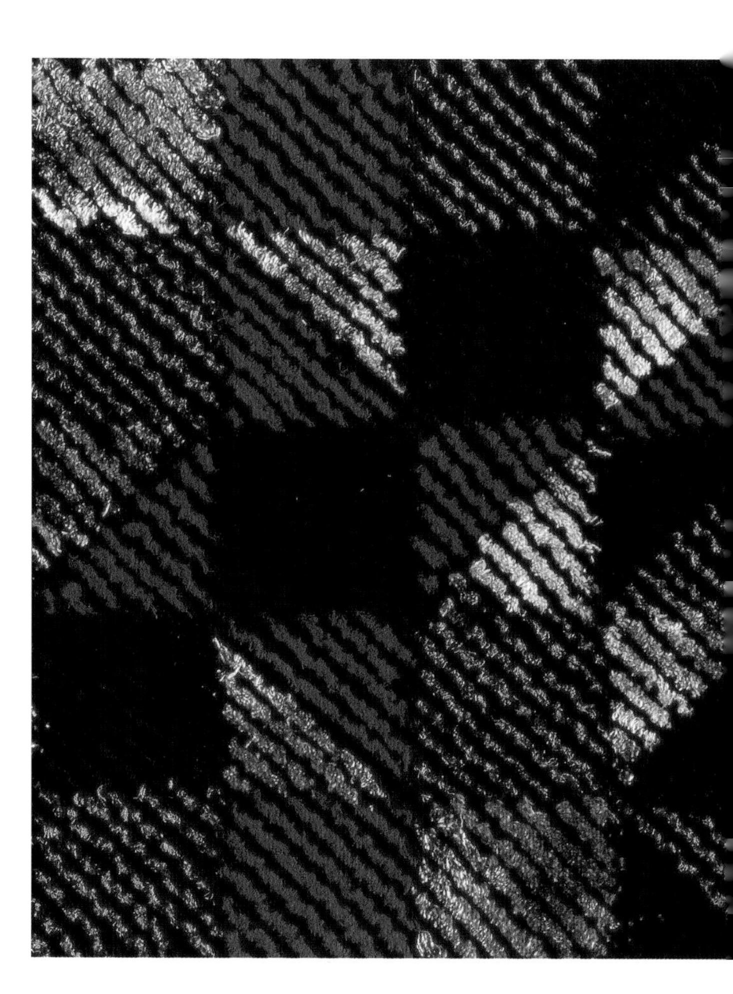

Chenille is adaptable to all styles of decor, as shown by these contemporary wall hangings.

Odyssey (top) by Peggy Neely, 29" x 40".

American Home Series: 21 Chassin Ave. (lower left) by Jack Brockette, 34½" x 46".

Cabin Fever (lower right) by Nannette Holmberg.

New Tools and Products

The main complaint from chenille makers is that traditional methods for cutting the top layers of fabric without cutting into the base layer are tedious and sometimes tricky. So much work is put into a project, not to mention the dollar value of the many fabric layers involved, that there was a tremendous fear of destroying such a laborious project in the final stages. Cutting was, at its best, the most time-consuming part of the procedure. I am happy to report that several products are available on the market today to assist you.

- **Cutting strips.** Cutting strips eliminate hours of arduous slashing with scissors. Just slide the narrow strip between the stitching rows and under all but the base layer of fabric, then cut through the upper layers with a rotary cutter. These strips are made from materials that will not dull the blade of your rotary cutter. Because the strips come in a variety of widths, you can slash wide channels as well as narrow ones.
- **Plastic strips.** The Japanese developed a plastic strip that can be inserted into narrow channels for use with rotary cutters. These strips look like tiny gutters that allow the cutting blade to run along the length of the strip without rolling off the side. They work well in very narrow channels, but in wider channels they tend to slide from side to side, which may cause uneven cutting. They are also short (7" long), and you must be careful not to roll the rotary cutter off the end (and cut into the base layer). The plastic may also dull the cutting blade.

- **Rotary cutter with plastic "track."** Another clever chenille tool is a rotary cutter with its own attached plastic track. For long narrow rows, this could be very fast and effective. However, its 2"-long track would prohibit cutting herringbone patterns or designs with directional changes in the stitching rows.

- **Wavy or pinking blades for rotary cutter.** Several books and patterns available now suggest using wavy or pinking blades in the rotary cutter to create chenille. These work well with pre-quilted muslin (see page 12).
- **Gluesticks.** When I made the ribbon jacket on page 19, I needed to fasten the ribbon to the fabric layers so they would stay in place while I was stitching the rows. Instead of pinning or tedious basting, I ended up fastening the ribbon by using a gluestick! Yes, I simply swiped the back of each ribbon piece with a water-soluble gluestick and stuck it in place. This securely held my ribbon flat while I completed the rows of narrow stitching.

Because of the glue residue on the back of the ribbons or scraps, it is necessary to add laundry soap or detergent (appropriate for the fabric combination) to the washing machine with the project. Failure to remove the residue will create areas where the ribbons are stiffer than the rest of the chenille; the result won't be completely soft and fluffy.

- **Spray adhesives.** New to the world of chenille, although not to the world of quilting, are spray adhesives. Quilters use some of these products to baste their projects. Spray adhesives can be great for sticking tiny pieces or scraps to the cutting layers and aren't as messy as gluesticks can be. Look for an acid-free adhesive that will wash out during the laundering process.

Some adhesive sprays will not only hold an appliqué securely in place, they will also allow you to reposition the shape without losing the sticking power until the piece is smoothed and pressed into final position. The repositioning doesn't leave a residue behind either, as the gluestick does. This gives you a chance to play with your design placement.

Cut to the Core (detail, opposite) by Christine Bramhall, 1999.

Spirals (right) by Christine Bramhall. This child's vest incorporates layers of denim and cotton prints. Circular stitching and printing interrupts the angled rows of chenille.

Reviewing the Basic Recipe

For some of you, this whole technique may be new, so you'll need the basic information presented in this chapter to make the projects presented later. For experienced chenille makers, you'll find this chapter a good review of the elements that make successful projects.

The basic recipe for chenille includes layering fabrics and quilting them at a 45° angle to the straight of grain. This creates perfect chenille—when you include the right ingredients. And testing is the only way to know if the ingredient mix is right. Creating chenille is not an exact science. I can't tell you to combine five or six layers of 100 percent cotton or 100 percent rayon and expect that you will have the same beautiful results you see in this book. It isn't quite that easy, but it is fun getting there. You must have an adventurous spirit and be willing to spend some time exploring possibilities.

You will increase your chance of success, however, if you follow a couple of basic rules. First, when you are testing for chenille or making a final project, *do not pre-wash any of your fabrics.* It doesn't matter if you are working with a fabric that typically shrinks; never wash your fabrics first.

Second, always make sample blocks (see "Sample Blocks" on pages 34–35). You might assume you would get the same results as in the book if you use similar fabrics. This seems logical, and in some cases will work, but why take the chance at ruining a garment when it only takes a few minutes to see exact results?

General Supplies

Making chenille doesn't require purchasing a lot of tools. In addition to basic sewing supplies, you'll need the following items:

- A sewing machine in good working order with an even straight stitch. It's nice to have a zigzag stitch if you want to add a decorative touch to the trims.
- Pins, pins, and more pins to hold the fabric layers together as you work. It's much easier to stitch and manipulate fabrics when they are pinned securely around the edges and about every three or four inches across the body of the piece. Pinning the layers helps avoid slippage as you sew.
- A rotary cutter and cutting mat. These are especially helpful for trimming the uneven edges of pieces that have been layered, stitched, and slashed.
- A 6" x 24" or similar size clear acrylic ruler with a 45°-angle line to use as a marking guide. The 45°-angle line is essential for marking the stitching lines.
- A 6" or 8" Bias Square® ruler or other square ruler.
- A marking tool, such as tailor's wax or a water-soluble fabric marker or pencil, for marking the stitching lines. You'll also need a marking pencil or a waxy marker that will not rub off for areas such as the center back (where you need to clearly see the pivot-point line for chevron designs). Tailor's chalk tends to rub off quickly and requires continuous re-marking. Tailor's wax or a sliver of hand soap work better.
- Blunt-nosed scissors for slashing the layers. There often are places where a rotary cutter and strips are not the best choice. For these areas, I use a pair of 8" bent-handled Gingher shears with blunt-nosed blades, which are less likely to puncture the base fabric than sharp-pointed dressmaker's shears.

Optional

- A walking foot, which allows the top and bottom fabric layers to feed through the sewing machine at the same rate, reducing shifting and puckering. It is useful when you're working with slippery rayons or other soft fabrics. You can find a walking foot for almost any machine. If you don't have one, alternate the stitching direction for each row when you stitch fabric layers together instead of beginning at the same edge each time.

- A quilting foot with a guide that can be set to several widths, to help you stitch rows a consistent distance apart. The drawback to this attachment is that you may need to sew on the same side of each row of stitching.

  Note: If you have trouble sewing quilting rows a consistent width apart, cut a strip of heavy paper (about the weight of poster board) to the width you desire and about 20" long. Place the strip next to the previous row of stitching and use it as a guide for the next row. Stitch right next to the edge for perfectly spaced rows.

- A basting gun, such as the QuilTak, which "shoots" little plastic tabs into the fabric to hold layers together, eliminating the need for pins. Many of my students have found this tool helpful.

Selecting Fabrics

Each fabric has qualities that are unique when included in chenille. Often, project patterns specify a certain fabric or combination of fabrics for the best results. I like to experiment, trying not to confine myself to any one fiber in any one project. I have achieved some of the most amazing results by combining a variety of fibers and textures.

The bolero jacket shown below includes a combination of fibers. The fabric stack in this jacket has rayon, raw silk, and a layer of tissue lamé with a base of soft satin. The jacket is detailed and bound with black velvet. One of the things that continues to amaze me about chenille is that I can combine fabrics like this in one fabric stack, with many of the fabrics being labeled "dry clean only," and then put them through the washing and drying process with such fantastic results. This evening jacket has such an elegant look and feel it is hard to believe that it's machine washable.

Bolero Evening Jacket by Nannette Holmberg, 1997. This elegant evening jacket has an unusual combination of fabrics. The base of soft polyester satin gives the stack of rayons, raw silk, and gold Lurex an elegant drape. The finishing touch is provided by rich, black velvet details and edge bindings.

Combining fabrics to find which combination blooms best is part of the fun of making chenille. But as I said before, there is no magic formula for selecting the right fabrics; each group of fabrics will react differently.

To create successful chenille, don't select fabric combinations the way you might for a quilt. Beautifully coordinated print and color combinations with comparable finishes and textures usually don't work for this technique. For chenille, combining fabrics that are totally unrelated in both color and texture often creates the most exciting results.

Approach chenille with an open mind. Try not to have a preconceived notion of what your final combination of fabrics will be. On some occasions your preliminary ideas may prove successful, but more often than not, you'll find yourself rearranging layers and adding or deleting fabrics in your sample stack until suddenly something works. It's good to be prepared for some combinations of fabrics that simply won't succeed as chenille no matter what you do to them.

So play around with your fabric choices and use the information in this section as a guideline only. It's what I've found as I've experimented with my own fabric choices, and while it may or may not have been successful for my purposes, you may have entirely different results.

Successful Fabrics

Natural fibers, such as cotton, linen, silk, and wool, are excellent candidates for chenille. However, layering fabrics of all one type can sometimes result in flat and lifeless chenille, so

Chenille Pillow Cover by Nannette Holmberg. If you've used a cotton decorator print to upholster a chair or sofa, use the same fabric to create a chenille pillow top. Although the print will soften when stitched and chenilled, it will still beautifully complement the original fabric.

try mixing a few loosely woven natural fibers together for splendid results.

Rayon, of course, is my greatest chenille discovery. Available in solids and prints, and in many wonderful colors, it is a great addition when worked into other fabric combinations. For soft, drapable chenille, incorporate a rayon challis into your recipe. Optimum results are best achieved by using only 100 percent rayon, although rayon blended with other natural fibers offers possibilities.

Look for fabrics with large, dramatic prints and a variety of colors. Prints that show good dye saturation provide the best color. When you turn many prints over to the wrong side, the back is almost white or gray and devoid of any sign of the print that is so beautiful on the right side of the fabric. These prints will usually disappear or fade completely after they have been stitched, cut, and washed. This is because the edges and much of the underside are exposed when the chenille is washed and dried. In some cases this muted background can give a soft effect that is very desirable.

The pillow top shown on the facing page is an example of a very dark print that blooms with a faded look but has the rich appearance of a watercolor painting after washing. It is possible to use the qualities of these fabrics to your benefit.

Ignore labels that proclaim "dry clean only"; they will only discourage you from using a fabric to its full potential.

Unsuccessful Fabrics

Synthetic fibers, such as polyester and acetate, generally don't work in chenille layers, no matter how great the color or print. Some, however, can be used for the base layer (see next column).

Avoid fabrics with a pile or nap, such as velvet, corduroy, and velour. They are generally too bulky. Some cotton velveteens will work fairly well when layered with other, softer fabrics, such as rayon. Fabrics that feel stiff or coated, even if they are marked 100 percent cotton, should also be avoided.

Stone- and sandwashed fabrics in general, even silk and rayon, will not be successful in chenille projects. This process changes the fiber, causing it to act like polyester.

If you feel you must use a fabric that just won't cooperate but has great color, layer it next to the base, or place it as the second layer from the base. Often the fabrics above it will help it bloom.

Secret Ingredients

To energize a flat sample of chenille, try adding one or more layers of the following fabrics to your stack. As you add fabrics, remove the same number of unsuccessful fabrics.

A loosely woven fabric, such as rayon mesh or cotton homespun, always adds texture and loft to a stack. One or more layers of gauze will also give chenille a wonderful texture. Gauze is available in a wide range of colors, or you can dye white or natural-colored gauze to the hue of your choice.

Needlepunched cotton batting will bring a stack of cottons to life, but it should be placed next to the base fabric.

In general, the addition of loosely woven fabrics, such as silks and fine woolens, produces a beautiful loft and soft texture.

The Base Layer

Because the base layer isn't slashed and doesn't need to bloom, you have more options than for the chenille layers.

The base layer becomes the lining of the jacket or vest, or ends up on the inside of a pillow or rug. Some of the fabrics in the unsuccessful category are suddenly okay to use for the base. Choose a fabric you like and want to see intact when you open your jacket. Keep in mind that a small amount of this layer will show on the outside of the project, between the rows of chenille.

Sample Blocks

The step that remains critical to the process is that of creating sample blocks. Using different fabrics and new techniques, it is more important than ever to make a series of sample blocks to test your fabrics before beginning a project. I can't stress this enough. I'm not saying that you can't take any three pieces of cotton, follow the procedure, and create chenille. You can. But if you fail to create sample blocks and don't experiment with more than one combination of fabrics, you will miss out on the best part of creating chenille: discovering the many possibilities. You may also miss out on the best possible combination of the fabrics you want to work with, and limit yourself to a narrow range of results. By not making sample blocks it is possible to end up with chenille that is less than wonderful.

Begin by selecting the fabrics you think you would like to use for the cut layers. I have chosen solid contrasting colors in cottons so that you can see the dramatic difference in the results when the layers are switched. Notice I always cut the base layers for my samples larger than the slashed layers. This is true whether I am making sample blocks or finished projects. If the base layer is at least 1" larger all around, it will be easier to find the lowest layer to cut as you slash between the rows.

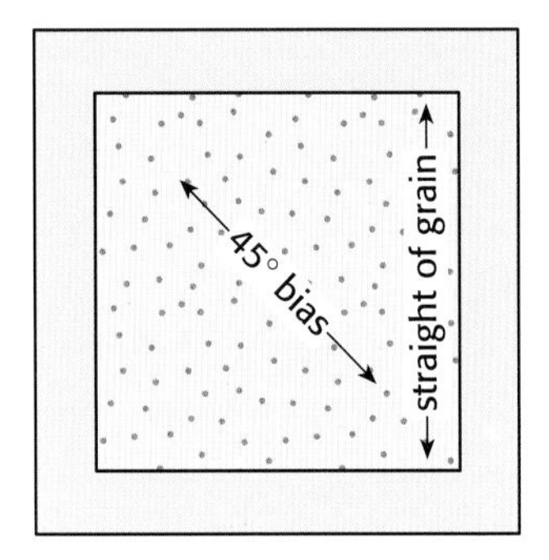

For the sample blocks, cut the upper layers into 6" x 6" squares and cut the base layer into an 8" x 8" square. Be sure that each square is cut on grain, so that the bias runs corner to corner. Now begin layering your stacks. Arrange the upper layers in a different order on each stack. For all-cotton chenille, try four layers—your base fabric and three more for the chenille stack. For rayon chenille, expand to a total of six fabric layers.

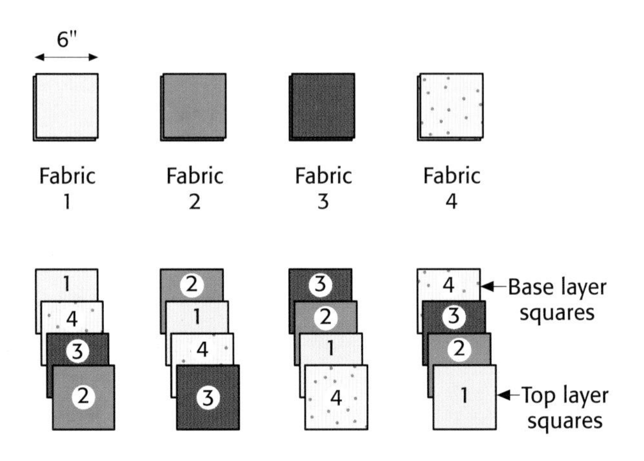

The base layer is the only layer that you can safely choose ahead of time because it won't be cut and will not effect the final fluff of the chenille. It is interesting, however, to see the top cut layers of chenille against a variety of lining or base colors. Again, the results may surprise you.

Once you've layered all your stacks you can begin stitching.

1. Place the base fabric right side down, then layer the remaining fabric squares on top, right side up. Pin the sample stack in a few places to keep it straight.

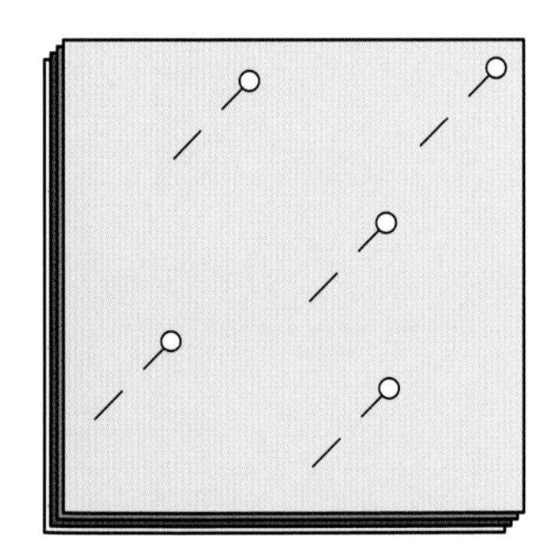

2. Using a ruler for accuracy, draw a line from corner to corner on the right side of the top layer. Move the pins if they are in the way of the ruler.

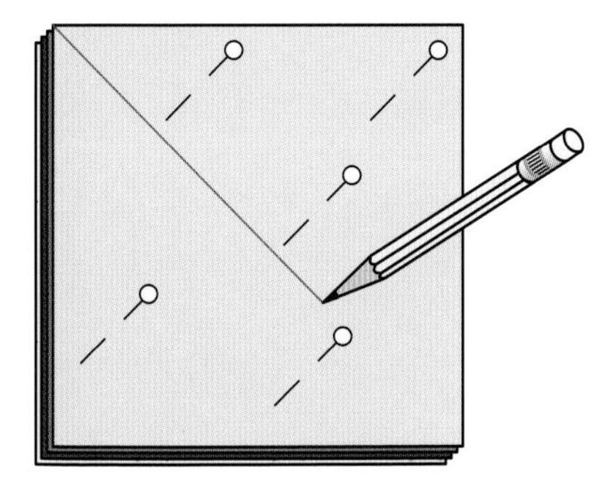

Tip: To make the stitching rows easier to see, select a color for the top thread that contrasts slightly with the fabric. For example, if the top layer is black, use a gray or navy thread in the needle. The stitching will be hidden after you wash your chenille.

3. Machine stitch along the line, using a stitch length of 10 to 12 stitches per inch. When using rayons, the rows of stitching work best ⅝" apart. Cottons work best when the rows of stitching are ¼" to ⅜" apart. Continue stitching, leaving the same distance between lines, until the stack is completely quilted.

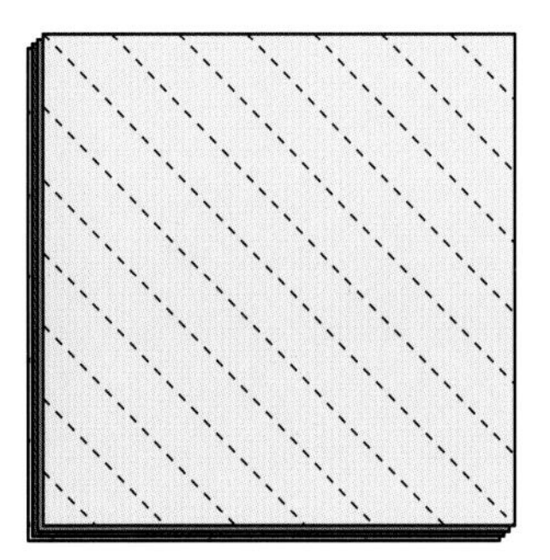

4. Cut all but the base layer between the stitching lines. Take care not to cut the base layer, or bottom, which must remain intact.

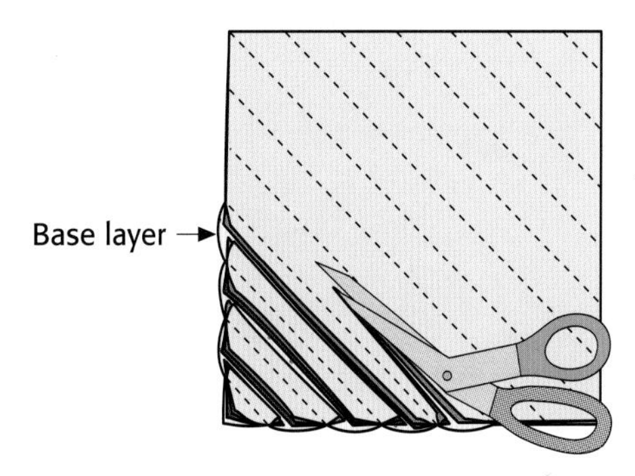

5. Launder the sample block, following the directions under "Laundering Chenille" on pages 38–39.

After experimenting with a pile of fabric taken from your stash, you are ready to move on. Now that you know what works well and what works even better, you can begin trying some new tricks and techniques to make your chenille more of an art form.

Stitch-and-Slash As You Go

Theresa Robinson of Viking/Husqvarna-White developed this technique for sewing and slashing chenille rows while working across the fabric layers. When the stitching is finished, so is the slashing! You will need an Omnistrip in the width you have selected for your chenille channels, an edge-joiner foot for your sewing machine, and a rotary cutter and cutting ruler. The edge-joiner foot comes with most machines and has a "blade" attached to it, making it look as though it is ready for ice skating. This blade runs along the edge of the Omnistrip, which acts as a stitching guide for the rows.

1. Layer the chenille fabrics according to the order you have selected from your sample blocks.
2. Turn the layers over so the bottom layer is on the top. Draw a 45°-angle line across the center of the layers.

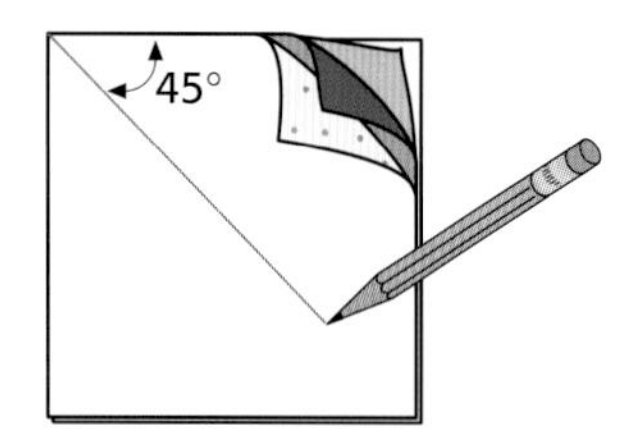

3. Stitch along the line you drew in step 2, through all the fabric layers.

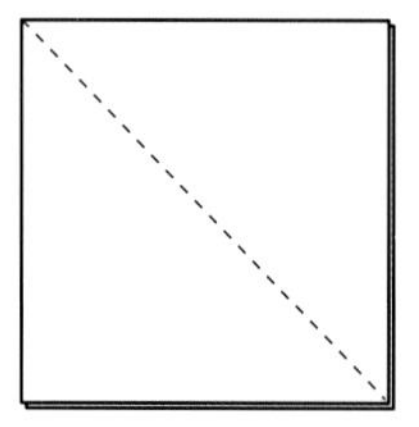

4. Lift the bottom layer only (now the one on top), and place the Omnistrip, gray side up, next to the stitching at the beginning of the row. Carefully place the lower layer back over the Omnistrip, smoothing out the layers.

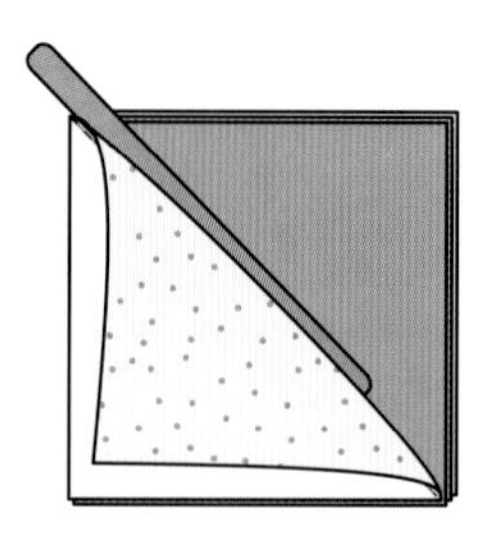

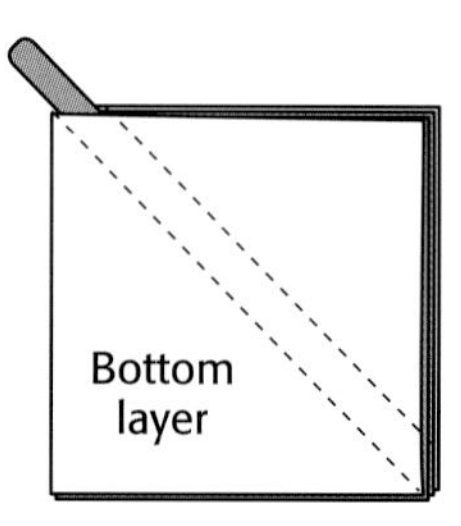

5. With the edge-joiner foot on the machine, place the blade of the foot along the right side of the Omnistrip. Move the needle position to the right so that it will clear the Omnistrip when stitching.

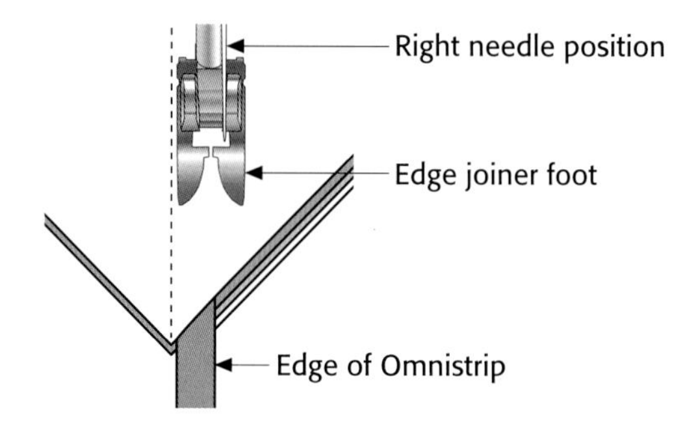

6. Stitch the second row of stitching, stopping to slide the Omnistrip farther down the row as necessary until you reach the end of the row. Adjust the layers as you stitch, taking care that all the layers are smooth and in place. When you are finished stitching the row, *do not remove the Omnistrip.*

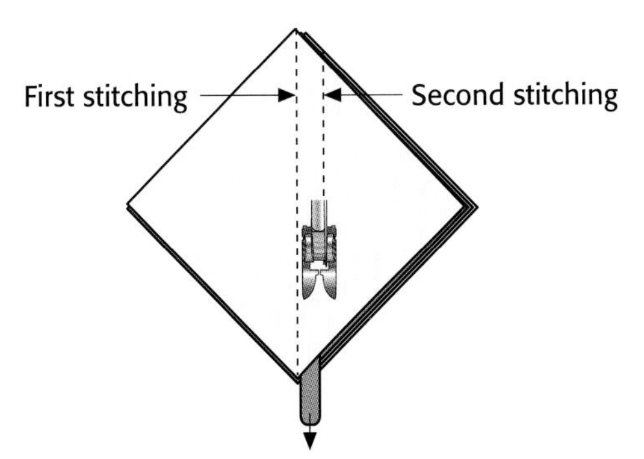

7. Remove the layers from the machine and turn them over. With your rotary cutter and clear acrylic cutting ruler, slash the top layers over the Omnistrip. If necessary, move the Omnistrip along the channel and slash until the entire row is slashed.

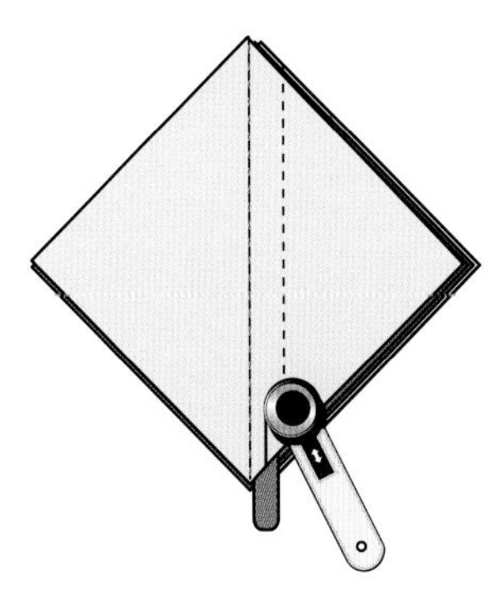

8. Remove the Omnistrip and turn the layers over to the back again. Smooth out the layers, and lift the bottom layer only and place the Omnistrip, gray side up, next to the previous stitching at the beginning of the row. Carefully place the lower layer back over the Omnistrip, smoothing out the layers. Stitch the next row.

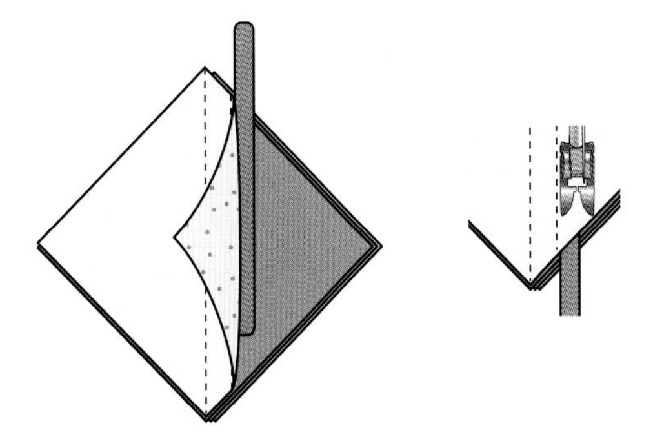

9. Repeat steps 4–8 across both halves of the project until the entire piece is stitched and slashed.

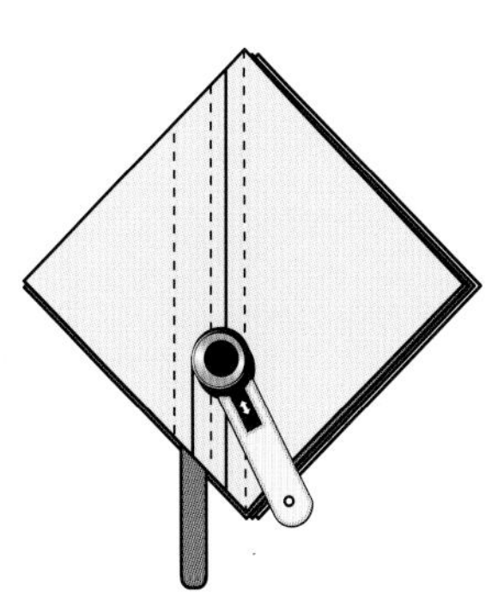

Note: While Theresa likes to remind her students to think of the gray side of the Omnistrip as the "stitching side" and the green as the "slashing side," both sides of the Omnistrip can be used for slashing.

Mending Cuts and Holes

Even when you pay careful attention to your work, accidents can occur when you slash your project. A hole may appear in the middle of your jacket, or you might accidentally cut an edge a few inches before realizing what you've done. Your first reaction will be to panic, but all your hard work can be saved.

First, measure the length of the opening. Cut a rectangle of base fabric 1" longer than the hole and 2½" wide. Cut a piece of fusible webbing the same size as the patch.

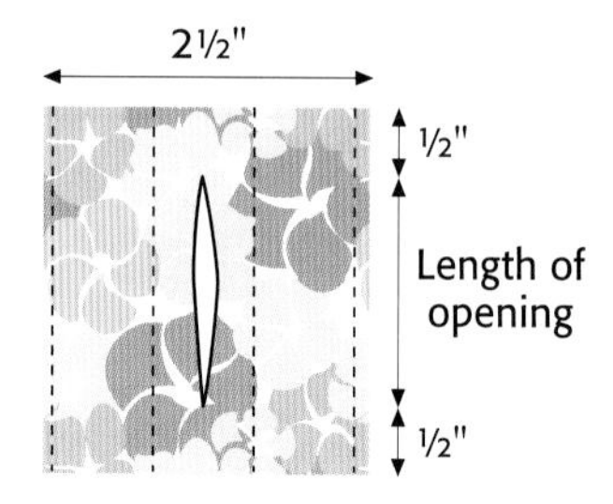

Following the manufacturer's directions, apply fusible web to the wrong side of the patch. When cool, peel off the paper and place the patch over the hole, on the inside (backing fabric) of your project. Center the patch ½" beyond each end of the cut and 1¼" to each side. Press to fuse.

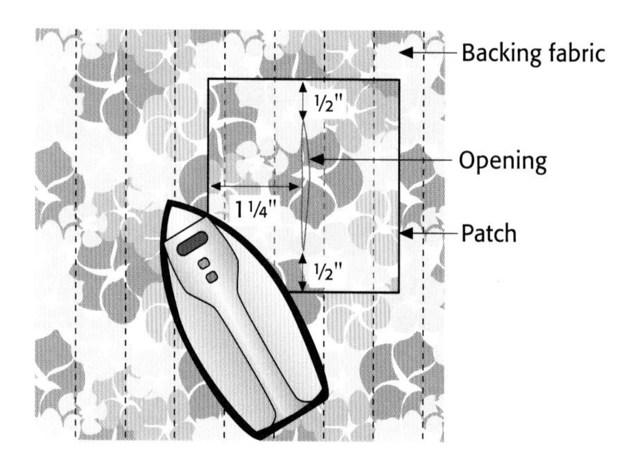

Turn the project right (slashed) side up. To reinforce the mending, sew on top of the stitching lines in the patch area.

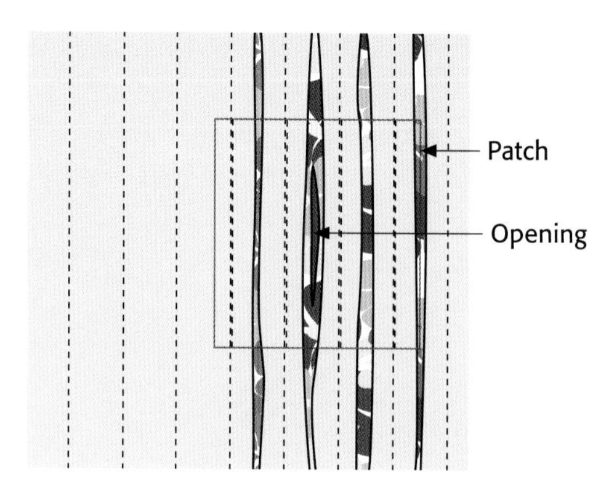

Note: If the mending piece is in a visible spot inside your garment, turn your mistake into a design detail by covering the hole with a cutout floral print or geometric shape. Fuse a few more flowers or shapes inside your jacket. Now you have designer details. Suddenly you're thrilled that the mistake happened!

Laundering Chenille

After you've cut all your stacks, they're ready to go through the laundering process.

1. At a sink, wet the blocks and wring them out. Hand agitate each block by rubbing it against itself until you see the rows begin to fluff up and separate from the base fabric. If your fabrics don't fluff—no matter how much you scrub the block—there's a good chance the chenille won't come up in the dryer either.

   Note: After wetting and agitating each block, you will find a huge mess of thread and lint in your sink. The same thing will happen in your dryer, so be sure your lint filter is clean before you dry the blocks.

2. Place the blocks in the dryer with a few old towels. Set the dryer at a medium setting, then check the blocks after 15 minutes. Don't remove them until they are completely dry.

A sample block ready for laundering.

Fluffed and separated rows

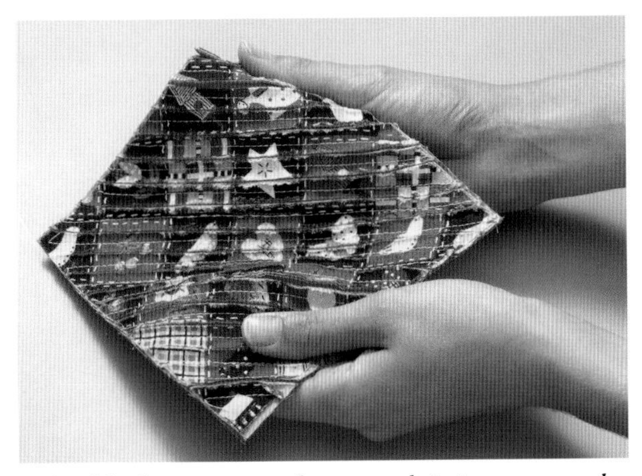

This block, no matter how much it is tormented, refuses to fluff or separate.

When the blocks go into the dryer, only the top layer of the stack shows, and the look of the block is rough. When you come back to the dryer in fifteen minutes or so (and if your fabrics have bloomed correctly), you'll be amazed at the metamorphosis that has taken place. You'll find yourself waiting anxiously by the dryer, as I do, to see the final results.

Laundering large pieces, such as garments or wall hangings, is similar to laundering sample blocks. Place the garment in the washing machine by itself. Do not wash it for the first time with other things because there will be a great deal of lint (more for some fabrics than for others). This lint will make a mess on the other items. Set the machine for a short cycle, regular or delicate, with a warm wash and cold rinse. I add about one tablespoon of detergent, but it's not necessary. I do it to remove any finish the fabrics might have.

Dry the piece by itself in the dryer at a medium setting. Be sure the lint filter is empty when you put your large chenille project in the dryer. It's a good idea to check the lint filter during the drying time too. The garment must be completely dry before you remove it from the dryer.

Clean the lint filter again after you remove the piece from the dryer.

Cutting and Applying Bias Binding Strips

1. Draw a line across the fabric at a 45° angle to the straight grain.

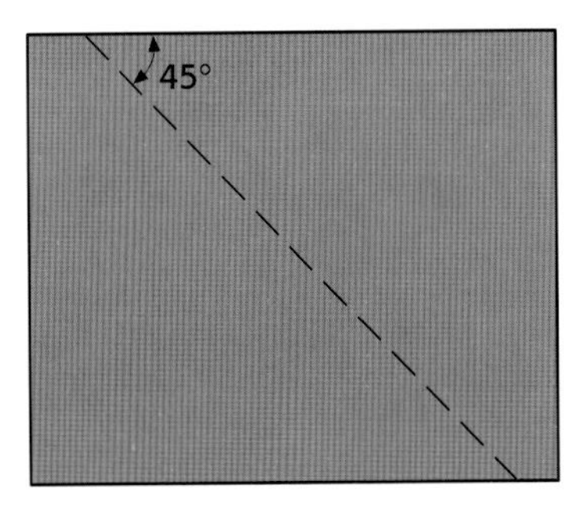

2. Using a rotary cutter and ruler, cut along the marked line. Cut strips of the desired width, parallel to the first cut.
3. Join the strips end to end until you have a strip of the desired length.

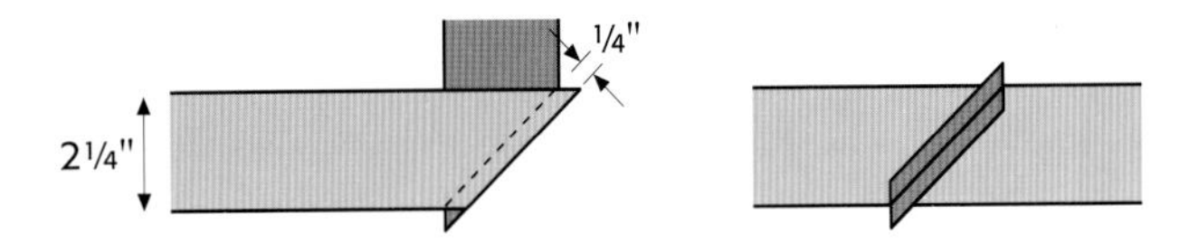

4. Pin the right side of the bias strip to the wrong side of the project. Pin the binding around the edges indicated for the project, mitering the corners.

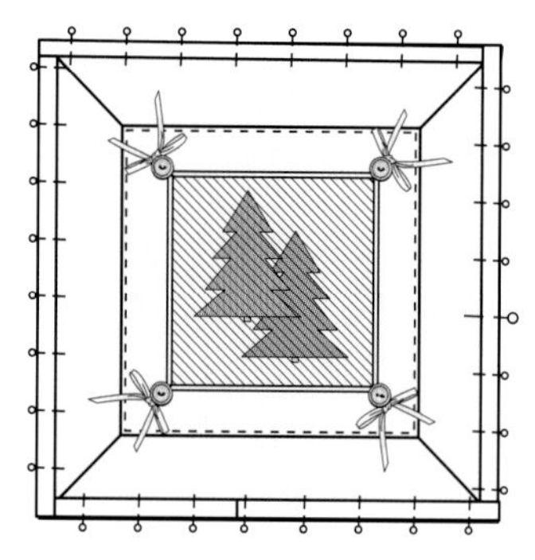

Binding the edges of a quilt

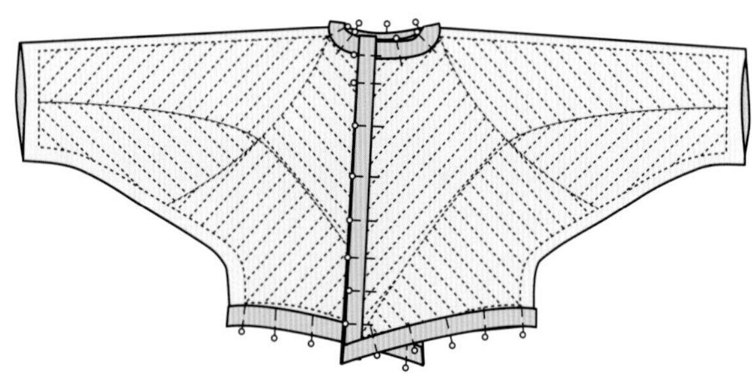

Binding the edges of a jacket

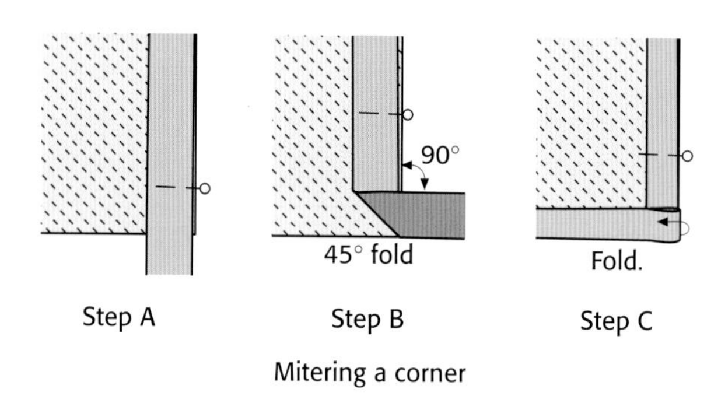

Mitering a corner

5. Overlap the binding where the ends meet. Turn under the unfinished end of the bias strip that will be on top when the binding is turned to the right side.

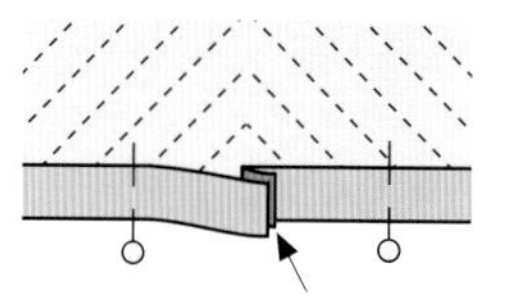

6. Stitch the binding to the project, using a ½"-wide seam allowance. At each corner, pull the fold of the binding away from the project and stitch to within ½" of the end. Remove the project from the machine and turn. Fold the binding back in place and begin stitching where the fold of the binding meets the project edge.

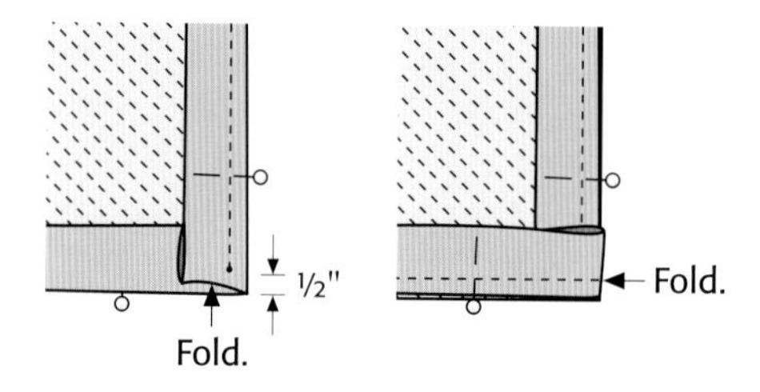

7. Turn the binding to the right side, folding it over the project edge. Turn under the edge and pin in place, using the stitching line as a guide. Stitch binding in place.

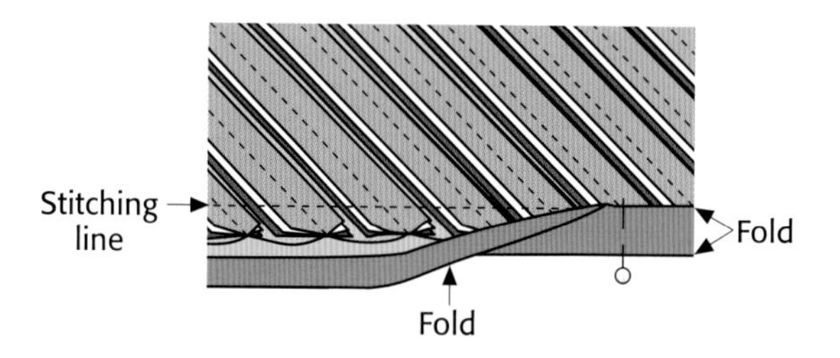

Projects

Selecting Garment Patterns

Slashed garments should be loose and larger than normal when you fit them—they will shrink when washed. The patterns in this book have been designed to accommodate the bulk created by the layered fabric and to allow for shrinkage. There are also commercial patterns available that have been designed specifically for slashed chenille jackets and vests.

If you want to use commercial patterns not designed for chenille, look for loose-fitting, unstructured styles. Dolman-, kimono-, and raglan-sleeve jackets can be adapted easily. The rule of thumb is to cut your jacket or vest two or more sizes larger than normal and add 1" to the sleeve and body lengths. It's wise to cut garment pattern pieces even larger and re-cut them to the final size after stitching and slashing.

Note: The patterns in this book are larger than standard pattern sizes to allow for shrinkage. Choose the size you normally wear.

The size designations in this book correspond to the following dress sizes:

Pattern	Dress Size
Petite	4–6
Small	8–10
Medium	12–14
Large	16–18
Extra-large	20–22

Preparing the Pattern

The patterns on the following pages are drawn on grids. To make your pattern, draw a grid of 1" squares on a large piece of paper, such as blank newsprint.

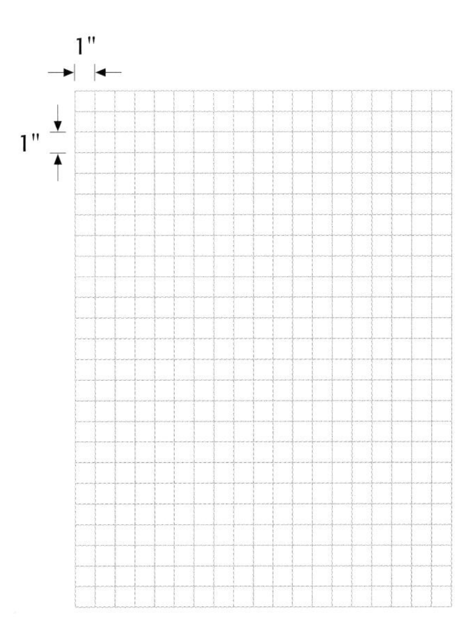

Transfer the pattern markings in the book to the corresponding square on your grid: one pattern square equals 1". If you are making a garment, take care to copy the correct size.

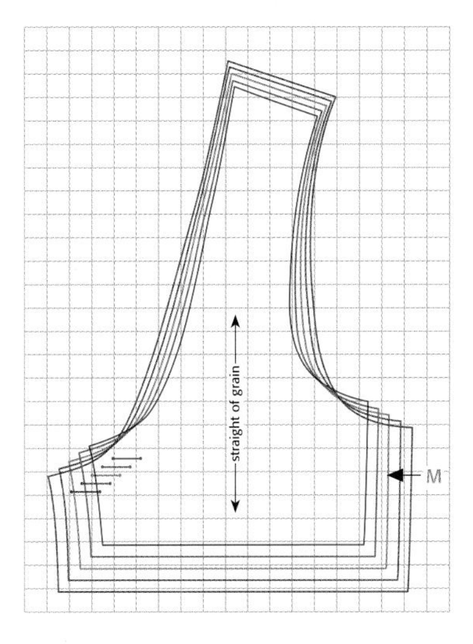

Asymmetrical Vest

This vest lends itself to every process in my chenille library because the lines are simple and unstructured. It can be casual or dressy and works equally well in any fabric. This particular interpretation features woven chenille. Yardage requirements are given for both cotton and rayon. Select the fabrics that give you the best results.

Yardage Requirements

Size	Piece	44"-Wide Cotton	58"-Wide Rayon
Petite	Chenille layers	⅝ yd. *each* of 4 contrasting colors*	⅝ yd. *each* of 4 contrasting colors*
	Chenille base and appliqués	⅝ yd.*	⅝ yd.*
	Left front and back	⅞ yd.	¾ yd.
	Binding, seam finish, and tie	½ yd.	½ yd.
Small	Chenille layers	⅝ yd. *each* of 4 contrasting colors*	⅝ yd. *each* of 4 contrasting colors*
	Chenille base and appliqués	⅝ yd.*	⅝ yd.*
	Left front and back	⅞ yd.	¾ yd.
	Binding, seam finish, and tie	½ yd.	⅓ yd.
Medium	Chenille layers	¾ yd. *each* of 4 contrasting colors*	⅝ yd. *each* of 4 contrasting colors*
	Chenille base and appliqués	¾ yd.*	⅝ yd.*
	Left front and back	1 yd.	¾ yd.
	Binding, seam finish, and tie	½ yd.	⅓ yd.
Large	Chenille layers	1 yd. *each* of 4 contrasting colors*	¾ yd. *each* of 4 contrasting colors*
	Chenille base and appliqués	1 yd.*	¾ yd.*
	Left front and back	1 yd.	¾ yd.
	Binding, seam finish, and tie	½ yd.	⅓ yd.
Extra-large	Chenille layers	1 yd. *each* of 4 contrasting colors*	¾ yd. *each* of 4 contrasting colors*
	Chenille base and appliqués	1¼ yds.*	1 yd.*
	Left front and back	1¼ yds.	1 yd.
	Binding, seam finish, and tie	½ yd.	½ yd.

**Do not preshrink.*

Supplies

Coordinating thread
¾"-diameter button
Water-soluble gluestick or spray adhesive
Tailor's chalk or water-soluble marking pen
9" square of paper-backed fusible web

Cutting

1. Referring to "Sample Blocks" on pages 34–35, make sample blocks from the chenille and base fabrics, weaving strips of the chenille fabrics as instructed in the directions that follow.
2. Following the directions on page 41, prepare the pattern pieces, including the stars.

   Measure the right vest front width and length at the widest and longest points. From *each* of the 4 contrasting colors, cut 1 rectangle that is 2" larger than the measured width and length. Number the rectangles 1–4 in the order established by the preferred sample block.
3. Cut strips from the rectangles, varying the widths from ¾" to 3":

   Colors 1 and 2: cut strips lengthwise
   Colors 3 and 4: cut strips crosswise
4. From the base fabric, cut 1 rectangle the same size as your chenille-panel rectangles (see step 2 above) for the weaving base. Cut another rectangle that is 2" longer and wider than the chenille-panel rectangles for the chenille base.

Chenille Panel Assembly

1. Apply glue in a ½"-wide strip to the left side of the weaving-base rectangle.

2. Starting ¾" from the top edge of the weaving base, place the crosswise strips (colors 3 and 4) side by side along the left side to form the weft. Alternate the colors and vary the widths. Press the left edge in place along the glued line, and reinforce with straight pins if necessary.

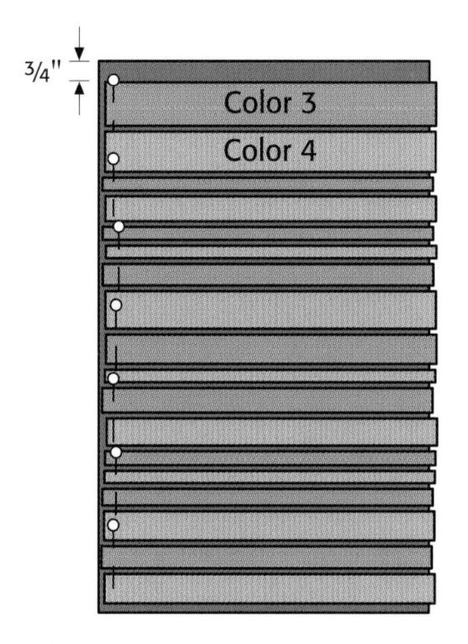

3. Fold the ends of the strips away from the base, being careful not to pull them loose.

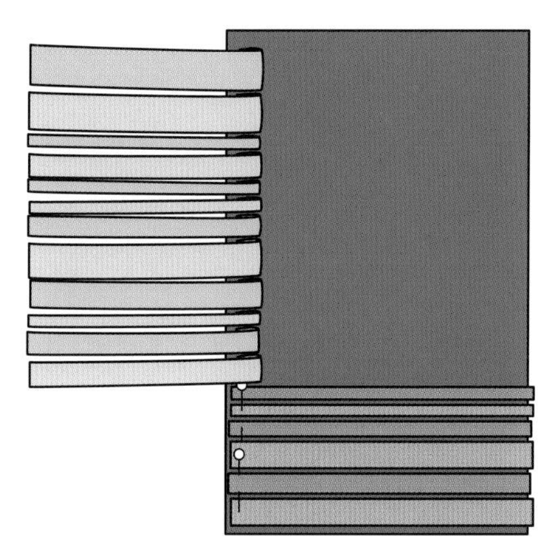

4. Apply gluestick across the top of the panel in a ½"-wide strip.

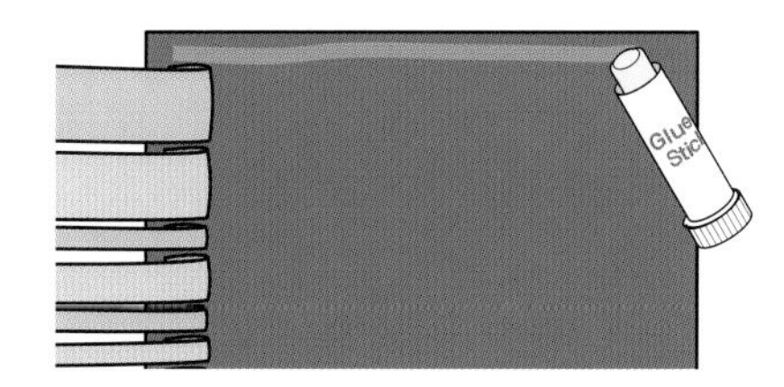

5. Starting ¾" from the left edge, place the lengthwise strips (colors 1 and 2) side by side across the top of the panel to form the warp. Alternate the colors and vary the strip widths.

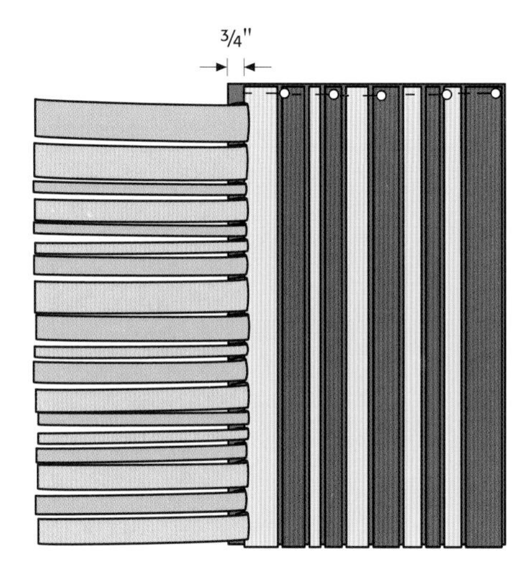

6. Bring back every other crosswise strip (weft), positioning the strips over the base.
7. Lay the first lengthwise strip (warp) over the weft.

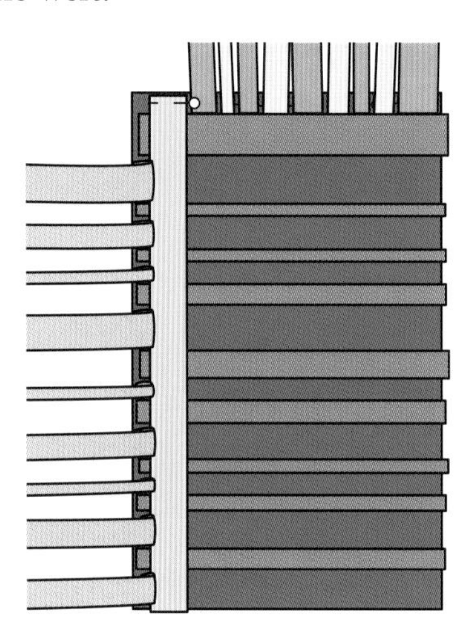

8. Bring the alternating weft strips into position and fold the first weft strips back to the left. Bring the second warp strip into place.

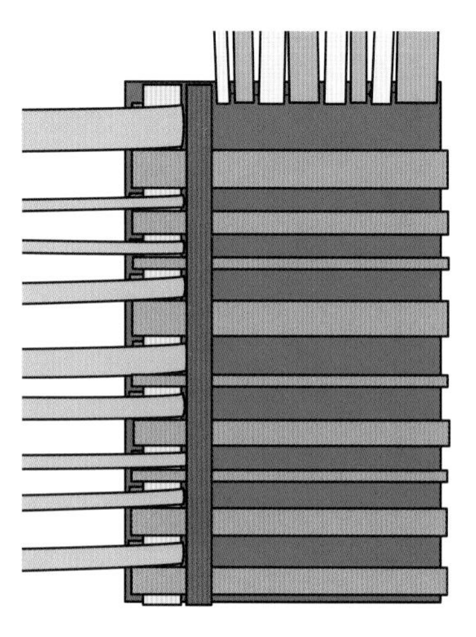

9. Repeat steps 6–8 to weave all the strips.

10. Draw a line at a 45° angle to the grain line of the fabric. This will be your first stitching line.

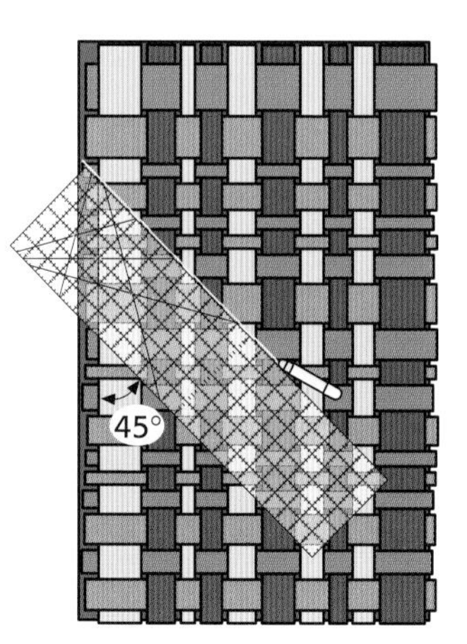

11. Center the woven block on the chenille-base rectangle, leaving a 1" margin all the way around.
12. Pin the woven block around the edges and randomly over the surface to hold the strips in place.

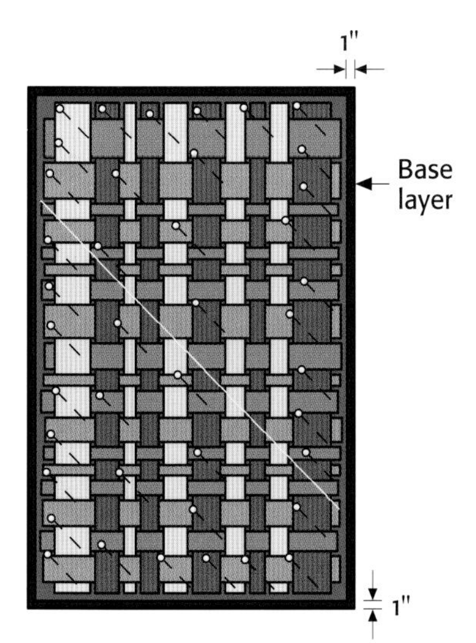

13. Stitch along the 45°-angle line you drew in step 10. Stitch a second row ⅜" from and parallel to the first. Continue stitching parallel rows until half the panel is quilted.

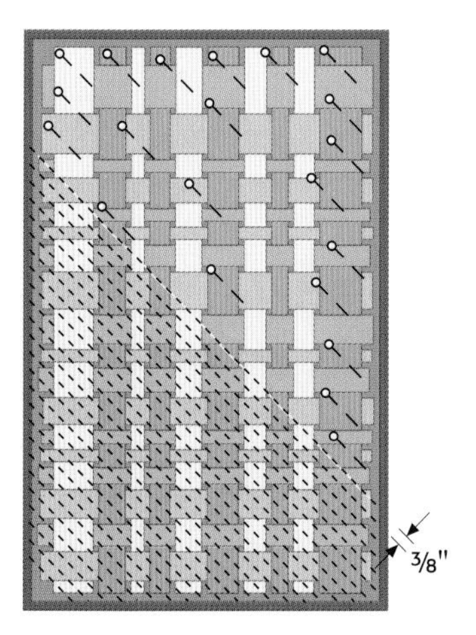

Note: The ideal width between stitching rows is ⅜". Wider channels reveal too much of the base layer, which means you lose the woven design. Narrower channels make slashing difficult and don't provide a deep pile.

14. Stitch the second half of the panel until it is completely quilted.
15. Taking care not to cut the chenille base layer, slash the top 3 layers (the 2 woven layers and the first base layer). Cut between the stitching lines, down the center of each channel, using scissors or a rotary cutter and strips (refer to "Sample Blocks" on pages 34–35 for basic cutting directions).
16. Wash the panel in a washing machine with a small amount of laundry detergent. Set the dryer at "permanent press" and dry the panel completely.

Vest Cutting and Assembly

1. Lay the right front pattern piece right side up on the fluffy side of the chenille panel. Align the grain as shown on the pattern to keep the woven plaid straight.

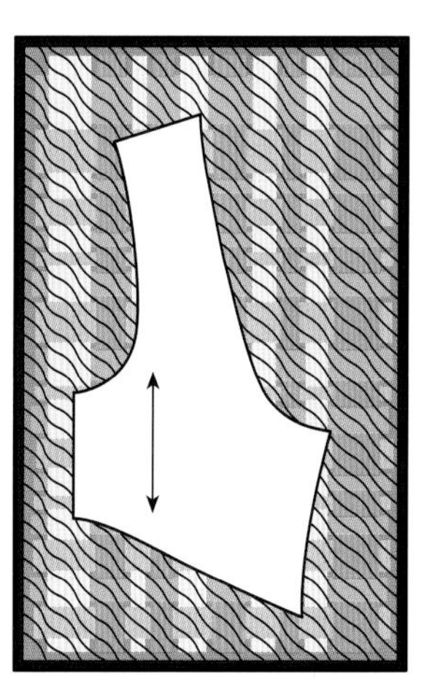

2. Cut out the left front and back from the vest fabric.

3. With wrong sides together, sew the vest fronts to the back at the shoulder and side seams, using a ⅝"-wide seam allowance. After stitching, trim the seam allowances to ¼", then press them to one side.

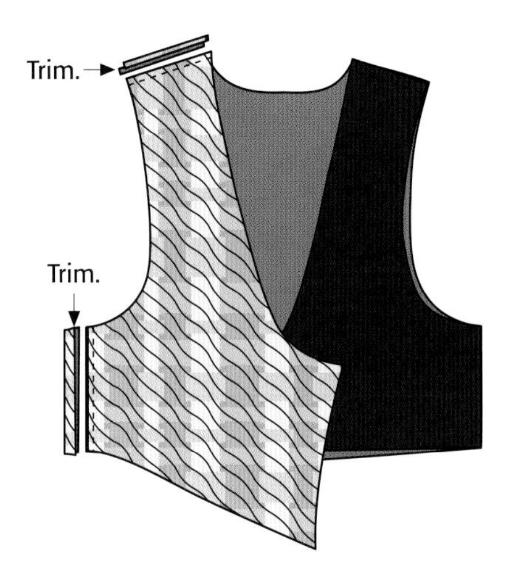

4. From the binding fabric, cut 2 strips, each 1½" x 6", for the ties.
5. Referring to "Cutting and Applying Bias Binding Strips" on pages 39–40, from the remaining binding fabric, cut enough 1¼"-wide bias strips to cover the shoulder and side seams plus 8". Also cut enough 2¼"-wide bias strips to bind the front, neck, and lower edges, and the armhole openings, plus 10".
6. Join the 1¼"-wide bias strips end to end, then press under ¼" along each strip's long edge to make finished bias trim.

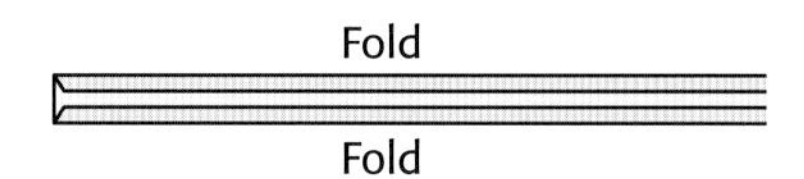

7. From the finished bias trim, cut 2 pieces the length of the shoulder seams plus 2". Repeat for the side seams. With the raw edges down, center the bias trim over the shoulder and side seam allowances and pin in place. Stitch close to the edge of the trim, first on one side then the other, removing pins as you sew. Trim the ends even with the garment edges.

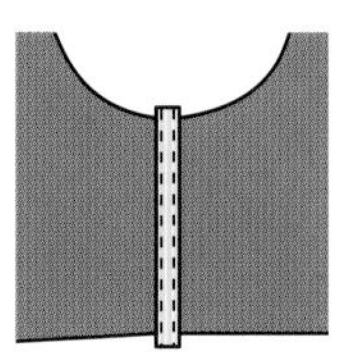

8. Join the 2¼"-wide bias strips end to end as described in "Cutting and Applying Bias Binding Strips" on pages 39–40. From the joined strips, cut 1 piece long enough to go around the neck, front, and lower edges, plus 2". Beginning on the inside lower edge, bind the vest outer edges, mitering the corners.
9. Edgestitch the turned under edge of the binding, then edgestitch the binding along the vest outer edge. The second row of stitching gives the binding a clean, professional look and keeps it crisp and flat throughout the laundering process.

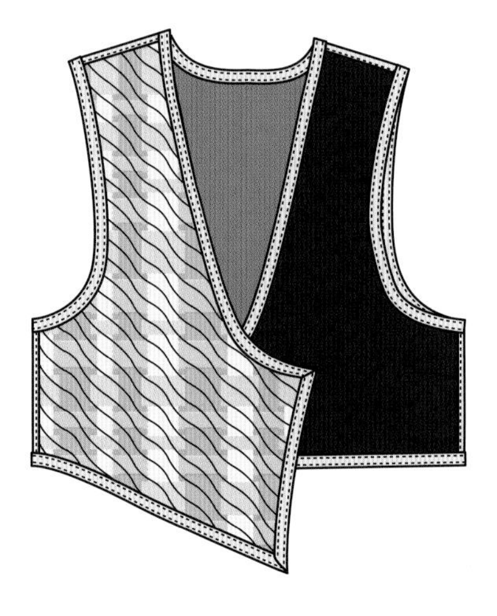

10. Bind the armholes in the same manner.
11. Trace the star templates you made onto the paper side of the fusible web. Cut out the stars ¼" from the drawn lines. Fuse each piece to the wrong side of the appliqué fabric, following the manufacturer's instructions. Cut out the stars on the drawn lines and remove the paper backing.

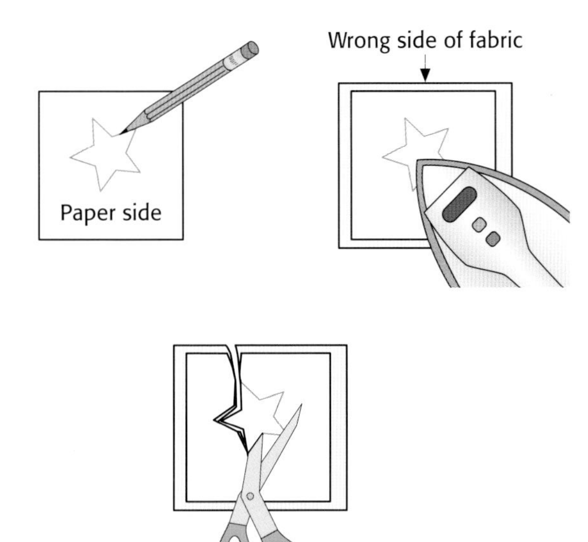

12. Place the stars on the left front as desired and fuse in place.

13. Finish the edges of the stars with either a machine satin stitch or a blind hemstitch (for a hand-embroidered look).
14. Stitch a buttonhole in the left front where indicated. Sew the button in place on the inside right front at the vest point.
15. With right sides together, fold each tie in half lengthwise and stitch ¼" from the long raw edge and across one end. Turn the tube and press.
16. Attach 1 tie to the point of the right front. Place the vest flat on a table, with the right front over the left front. Attach the second tie ¾" to the right of where the right front's point touches the left vest front.

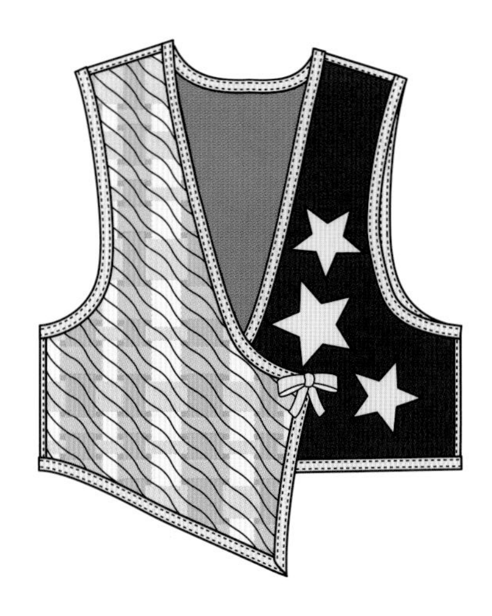

Vest Variation

Woven-Ribbon Vest by Nannette Holmberg. Give your vest a sophisticated twist by replacing the woven fabric strips with silk ribbon.

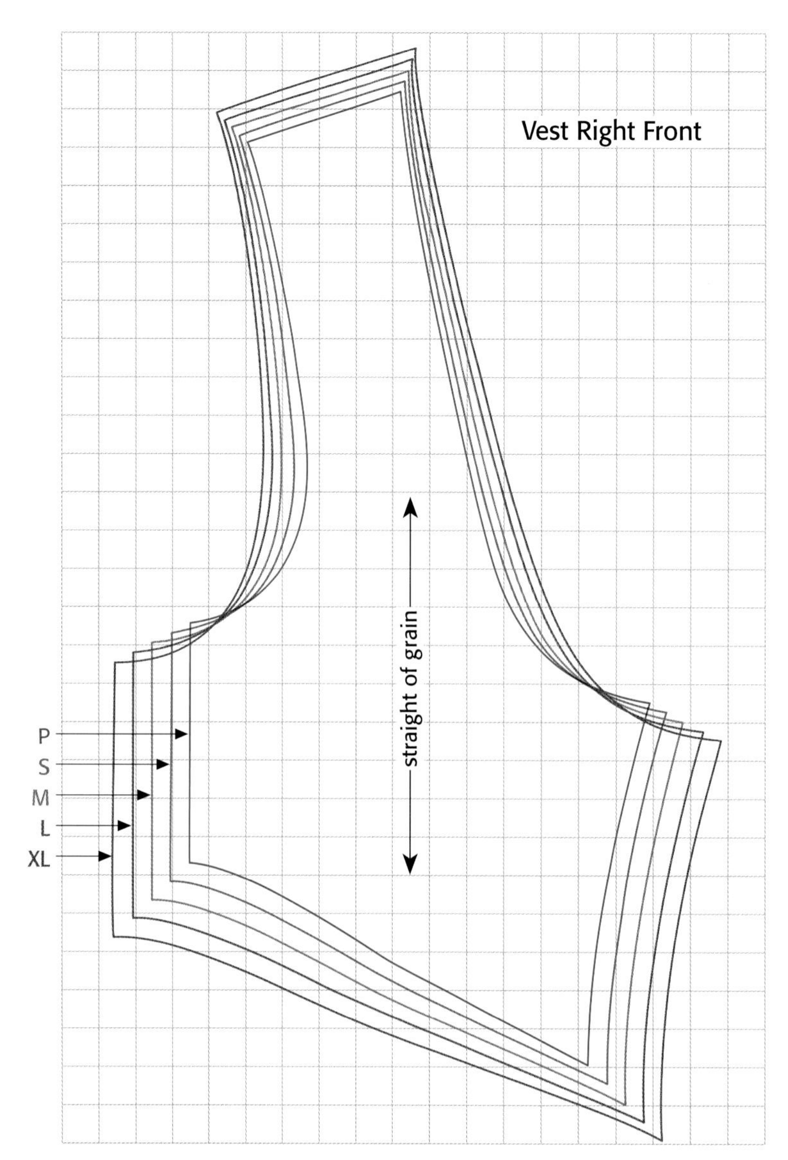

1 square = 1"

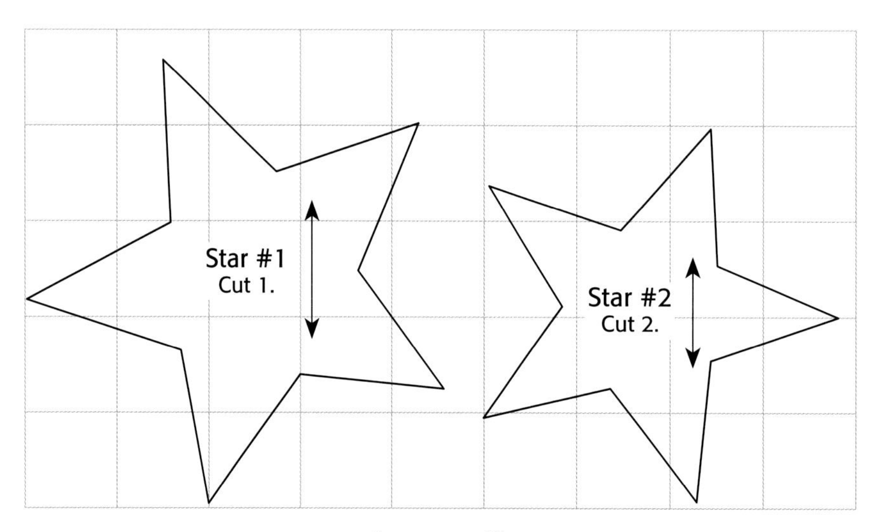

1 square = 1"

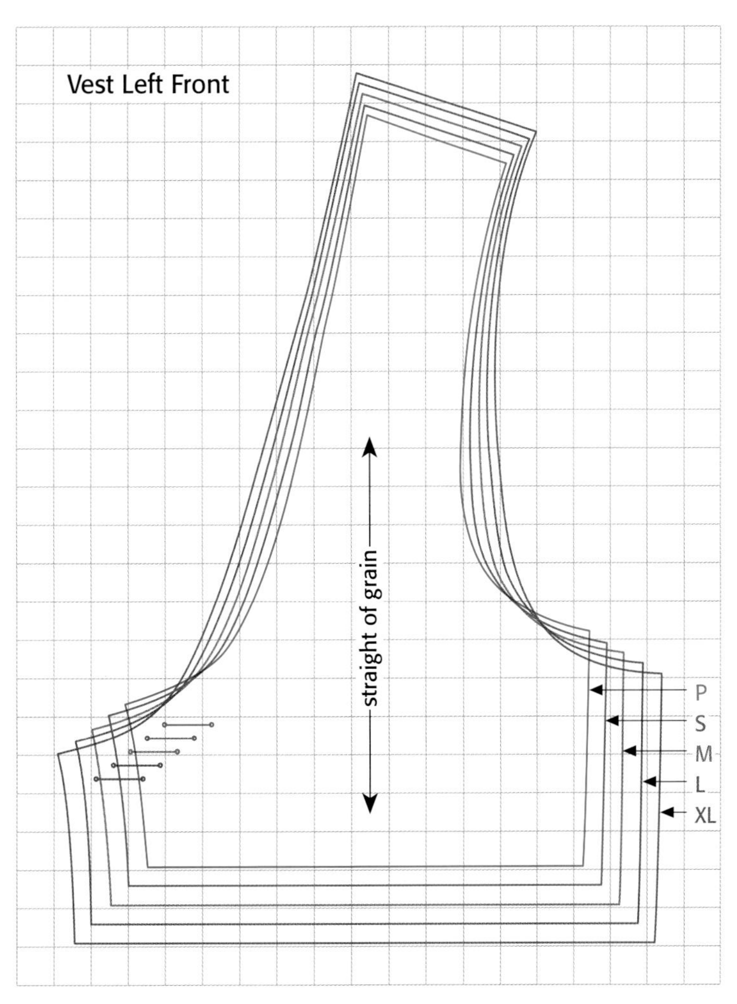

1 square = 1"

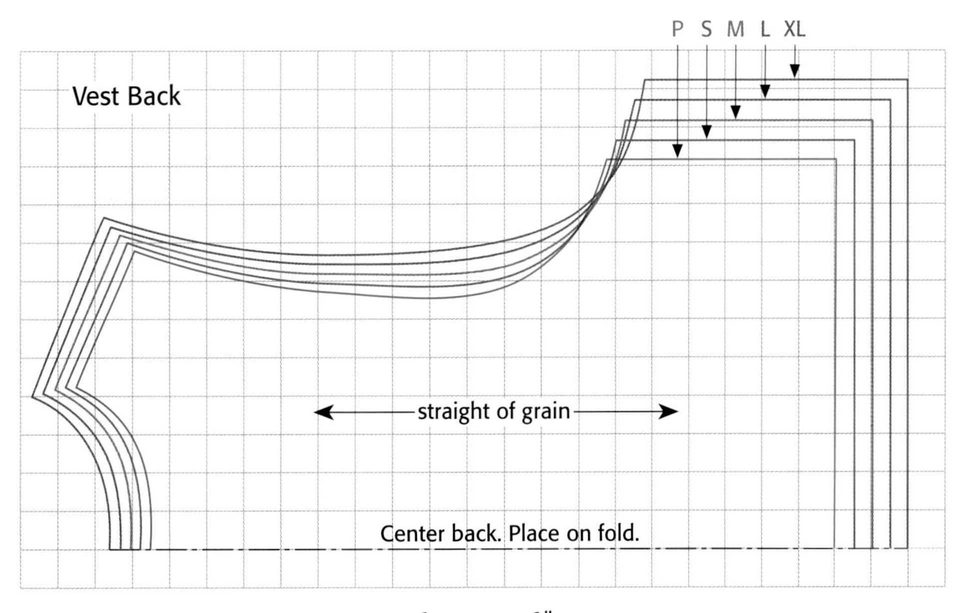

1 square = 1"

Two-Color Cotton Jacket

Since the publication of my first book, Variations in Chenille, *I have had numerous requests for the jacket featured on the front and back covers of the book. When I received letters of disappointment from as far away as Europe, I finally agreed to release the pattern for my most popular jacket. The jacket is included here to make for your personal enjoyment but may not be reproduced commercially.*

The lines of this jacket are flattering and create a wonderful canvas for many of the procedures discussed in this book. I love to develop areas of contrasting colors and textures within the divided design areas.

Yardage Requirements

Note: Do not pre-shrink the fabrics for this project. Separate yardage requirements are given for colorations A and B, but you could use the same 3 fabrics for both colorations and simply change the order of the chenille stacks.

Size	Piece	44"-Wide Cotton
Petite	Chenille coloration A	1⅜ yds. *each* of 3 colors
	Chenille coloration B	1⅜ yds. *each* of 3 colors
	Chenille base	3¼ yds.
	Binding	½ yd.
Small	Chenille coloration A	1½ yds. *each* of 3 colors
	Chenille coloration B	1½ yds. *each* of 3 colors
	Chenille base	3⅜ yds.
	Binding	½ yd.
Medium	Chenille coloration A	1½ yds. *each* of 3 colors
	Chenille coloration B	1½ yds. *each* of 3 colors
	Chenille base	3½ yds.
	Binding	½ yd.
Large	Chenille coloration A	1½ yds. *each* of 3 colors
	Chenille coloration B	1½ yds. *each* of 3 colors
	Chenille base	3⅝ yds.
	Binding	½ yd.
Extra-large	Chenille coloration A	1⅞ yds. *each* of 3 colors
	Chenille coloration B	1⅞ yds. *each* of 3 colors
	Chenille base	3¾ yds.
	Binding	½ yd.

Supplies

Coordinating thread
1½"-diameter button
1 yd. of cotton cording
Tailor's chalk
Water-soluble marking pen or pencil

Cutting

1. Referring to "Sample Blocks" on pages 34–35, make sample blocks from your chenille and base fabrics. Use the same base fabric for each coloration. Select the 2 best combinations and label them A and B.
2. Prepare the pattern pieces for your size according to the directions on page 43, being sure to transfer the grain lines for each section. It is critical to position the grain line properly when you cut out the chenille layers.
3. Cut out 2 paper patterns each for your jacket front and back. Keep 1 pattern intact. Cut the second pattern along the design lines to yield 8 pieces: 4 for the jacket front and 4 for the jacket back.

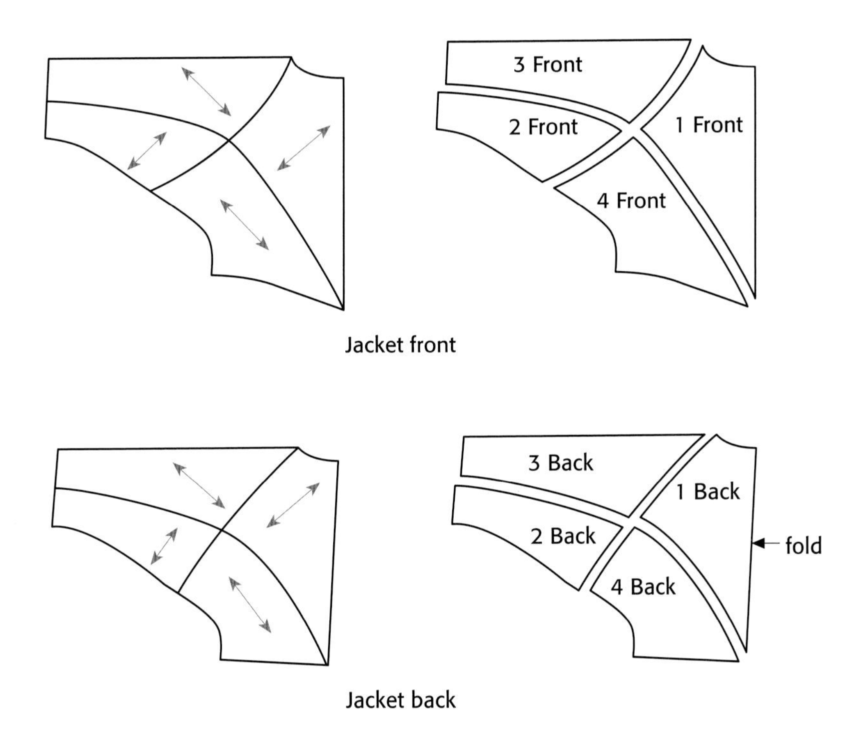

4. Cut out the base layers for the jacket front, back, and collar, cutting 1" from the edge of each pattern piece.

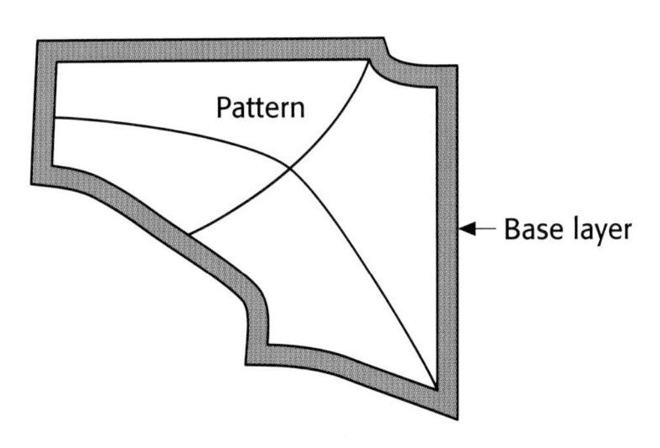

5. Referring to your sample block for coloration A, stack the chenille fabrics and cut out the collar and sections 1 and 2 for the jacket front and back.

6. Referring to your sample block for coloration B, stack the chenille fabrics and cut out sections 3 and 4 for the jacket front and back.

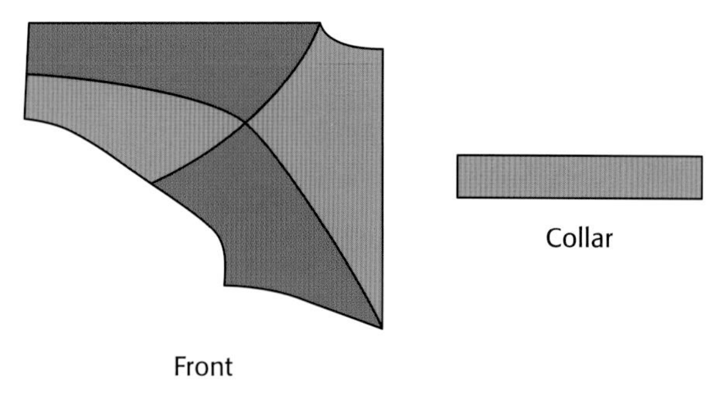

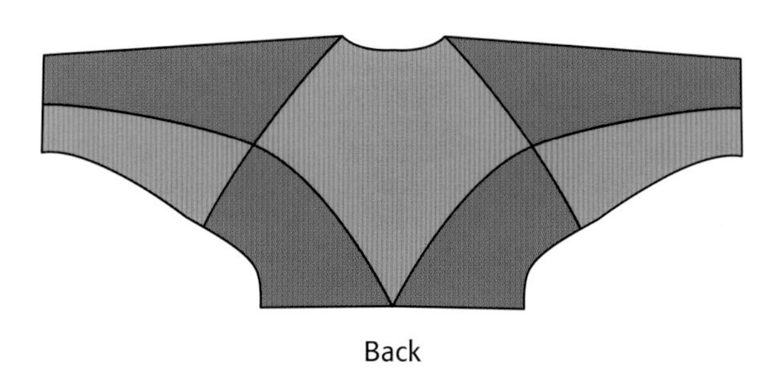

Chenille Assembly

1. Pin the jacket sections to the base layers as shown, butting the edges together.

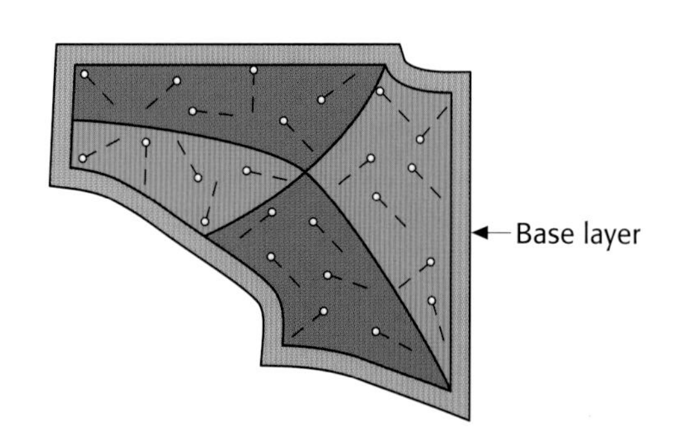

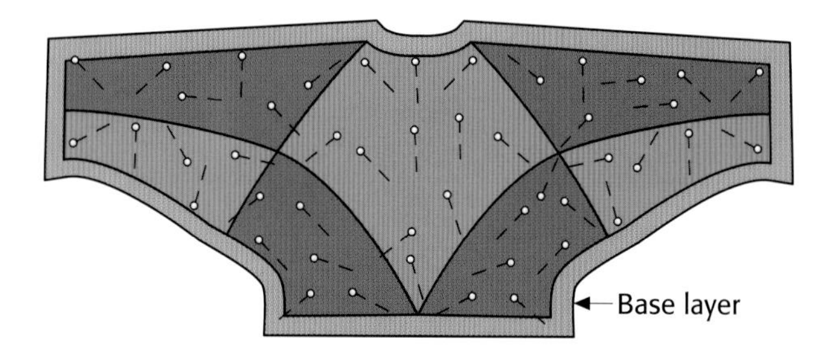

2. Chalk-mark a line at a 45° angle to the grain line on each section as shown. These will be your first stitching lines. Note that the stitching directions alternate between quadrants.

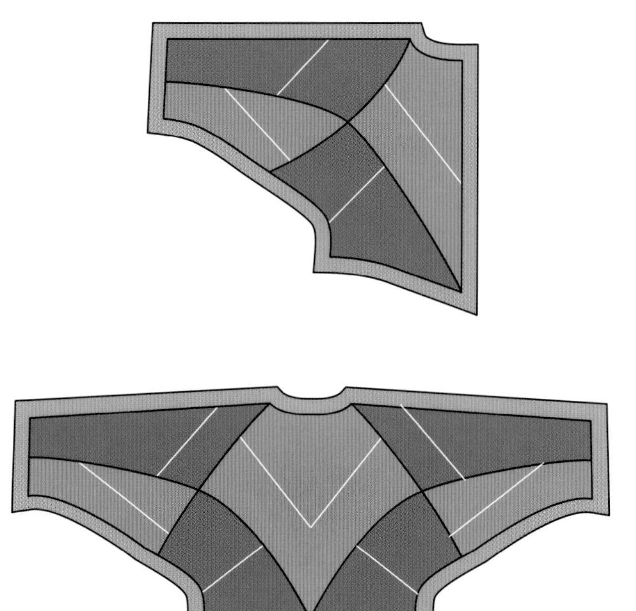

3. For each section, stitch along the drawn line, then stitch parallel rows 3/8" apart. Stitch each jacket section individually. When one area is filled with stitching, move to the next. When stitching the back, start with the center section and then stitch the sides.

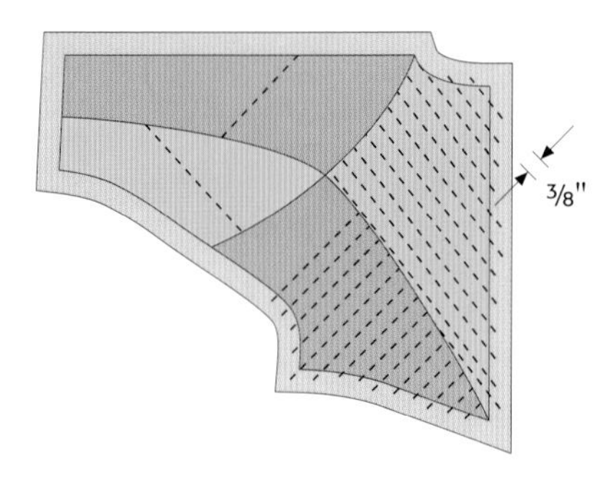

Tip: You may wish to roll up sections of the jacket that you are not working on and pin them securely to keep them out of your way while you stitch, especially for the back.

4. For the collar, center the 3 chenille layers on top of the base layer.
5. Using the fabric pen or pencil, draw a line down the center of the collar as shown. Mark lines at 45° angles from each side of the center line, forming a V. Stitch along one of the lines, then continue stitching rows ⅜" apart on both sides of the 45° line until that half of the collar is completely quilted. Stitch the other half in the same manner.

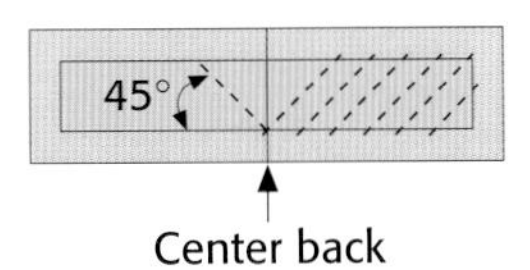

6. Taking care not to cut the base layer, slash the top 3 layers of all the pieces. Cut between the stitching lines, down the center of each channel, using scissors or a rotary cutter and strips (refer to "Sample Blocks" on pages 34–35 for cutting directions).

   Note: Channels that begin at the outside edges are easily slashed. In some areas, especially the center back, there aren't any outside edges to access. For these channels, start cutting by carefully clipping through 1 layer at a time with a pair of small, sharp scissors. Keep one hand under the layers to make sure you are not going all the way through. After cutting through the top 3 layers, slide your scissors blade or strips into the channel (above the base layer) and slash the row.

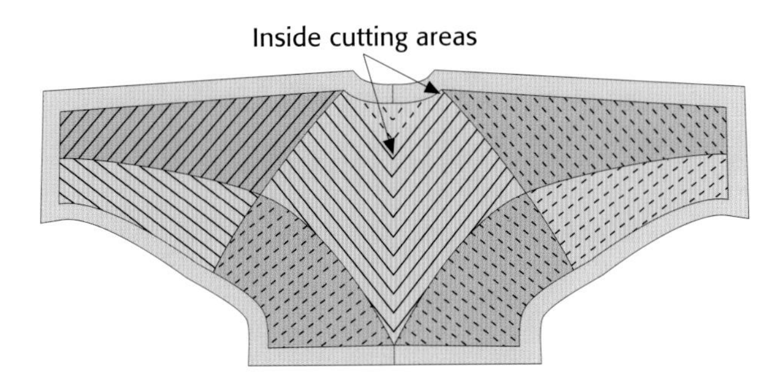

7. Once the jacket is completely slashed, lay the intact pattern piece (from step 3 of "Cutting" on page 55) on top of its section. Trim the excess fabric.

Jacket Assembly

1. Referring to "Cutting and Applying Bias Binding Strips" on pages 39–40, from the binding fabric, cut enough 1¼"-wide bias strips to cover the shoulder seams, the inside and outside collar seams, and the butted edges between each jacket section, plus an additional 32". Also cut enough 2¼"-wide bias strips to bind the neck, front, lower edges, and sleeve edges, plus 4".
2. Join the 1¼"-wide bias strips end to end as needed. Press under ¼" along each long edge to make a finished piece of bias trim.

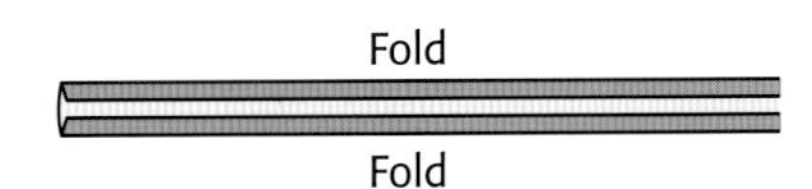

3. Cut and pin the trim over the butted edges where the colors join. Stitch in place along both edges, removing pins as you sew.

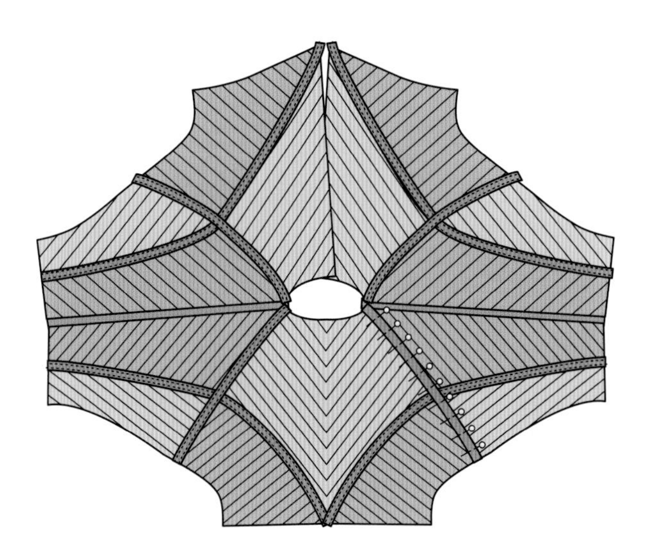

4. With wrong sides together, sew the jacket fronts to the back at the shoulder seams, using a ⅝"-wide seam allowance. After stitching, trim the seam allowances to ¼", then press them to one side.

Press trimmed seam to one side.

5. From the finished bias trim, cut 2 pieces the length of the shoulder seams plus 2". With the raw edges down, center the bias trim over the shoulder seam allowances and pin it in place. Stitch close to the edge of the trim, first on one side then the other, removing pins as you sew. Trim the ends even with the garment edges.
6. With wrong sides together, sew the side seams with a ⅝"-wide seam allowance. Trim the seams to ¼". These seams are now finished. I prefer to leave them unbound so they'll remain soft and become part of the chenille after washing. They may need to be trimmed a little after washing, but they will blend into the chenille.

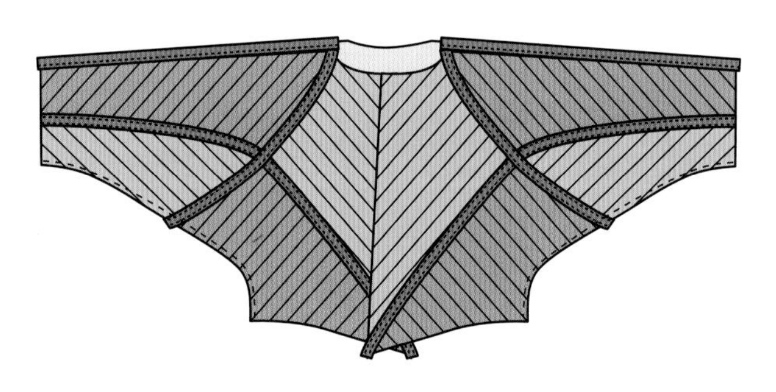

7. Lap the edge of the collar's ⅝" seam line to the ⅝" seam line on the jacket's neck edge. Zigzag the collar into place. Trim the excess fabric from the inside, as shown.

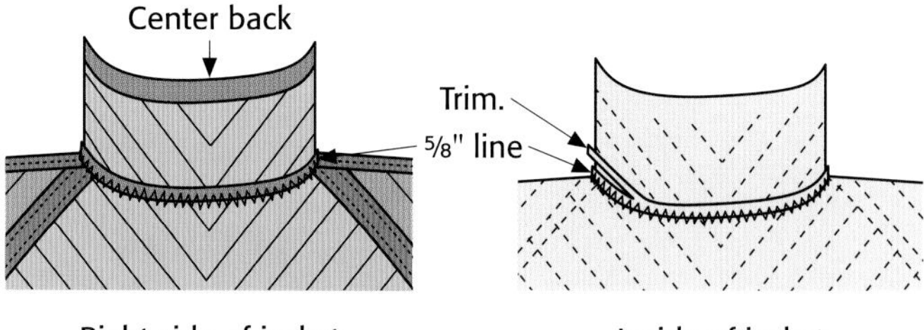

8. From the finished bias trim, cut 2 strips the length of the collar seam. Pin 1 strip to the collar seam on the inside of the jacket. Edgestitch the same as you did in step 4 for finishing the shoulder seams. Trim the excess even with the neck edge. Repeat for the outside collar seam.

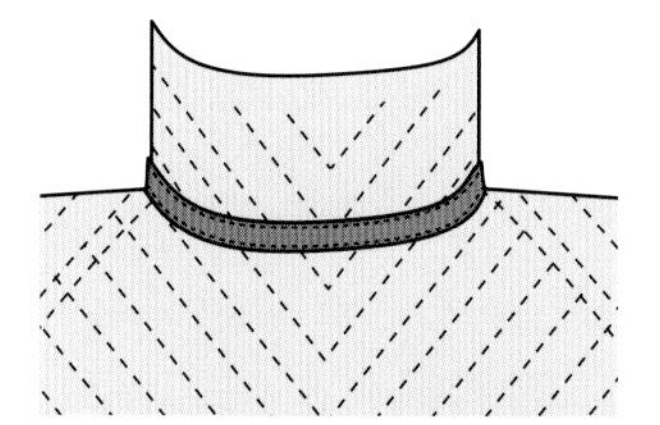

Right side of jacket

9. Refer to "Cutting and Applying Bias Binding Strips" on pages 34–40 to join the 2¼"-wide bias strips end to end until you have a strip long enough to go around the neck, front, and lower edges, plus 8". Turn under ¼" on one end of the binding strip.
10. Stitch the binding to the jacket, beginning at the inside lower edge and mitering the corners as you go.
11. Bind the sleeve lower edges in the same manner, using 2¼"-wide bias strips.
12. Wash and dry your jacket, being sure to dry it completely.

Jacket Closure

1. Cut a 16"-long strip of 1¼"-wide bias trim. Cut a 32½"-long piece of cotton cording.
2. Wrap the right side of the strip around the cording as shown, leaving 16" uncovered at one end. Using a zipper foot attachment on your sewing machine, stitch close to the cording. Sew across the short end of the fabric, over the cording.

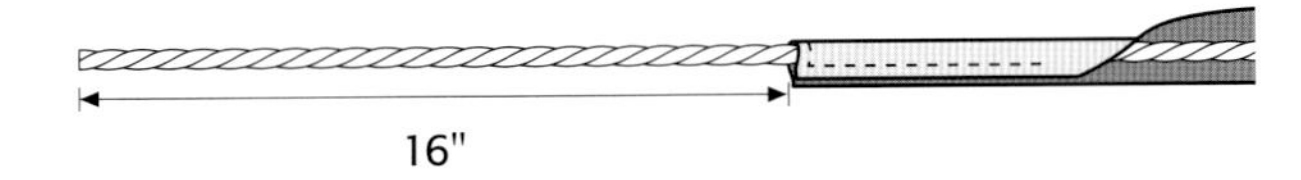

3. Trim the seam allowance to ⅛". Pull the fabric over the uncovered cording. Cut off the uncovered cording.

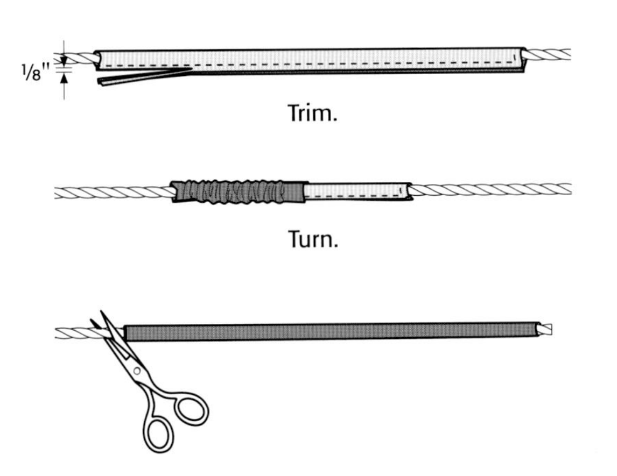

4. Make a pattern with the cording as shown, stitching the cords together where they overlap. Stitch the cording just below the collar on the right front of the jacket.

5. Lap the right jacket front over the left front and mark the button placement.
6. Sew the button on the left jacket front.

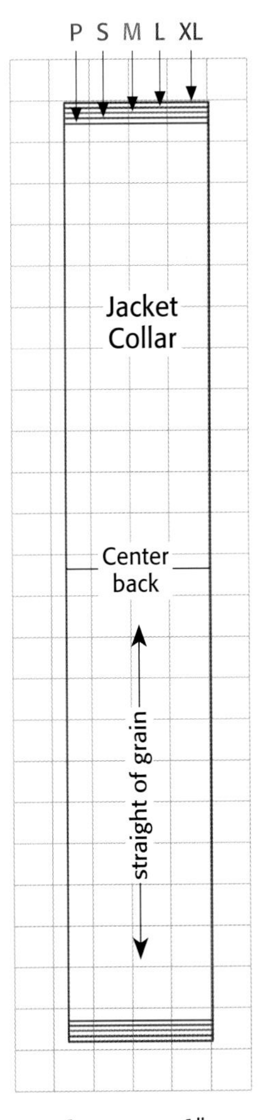

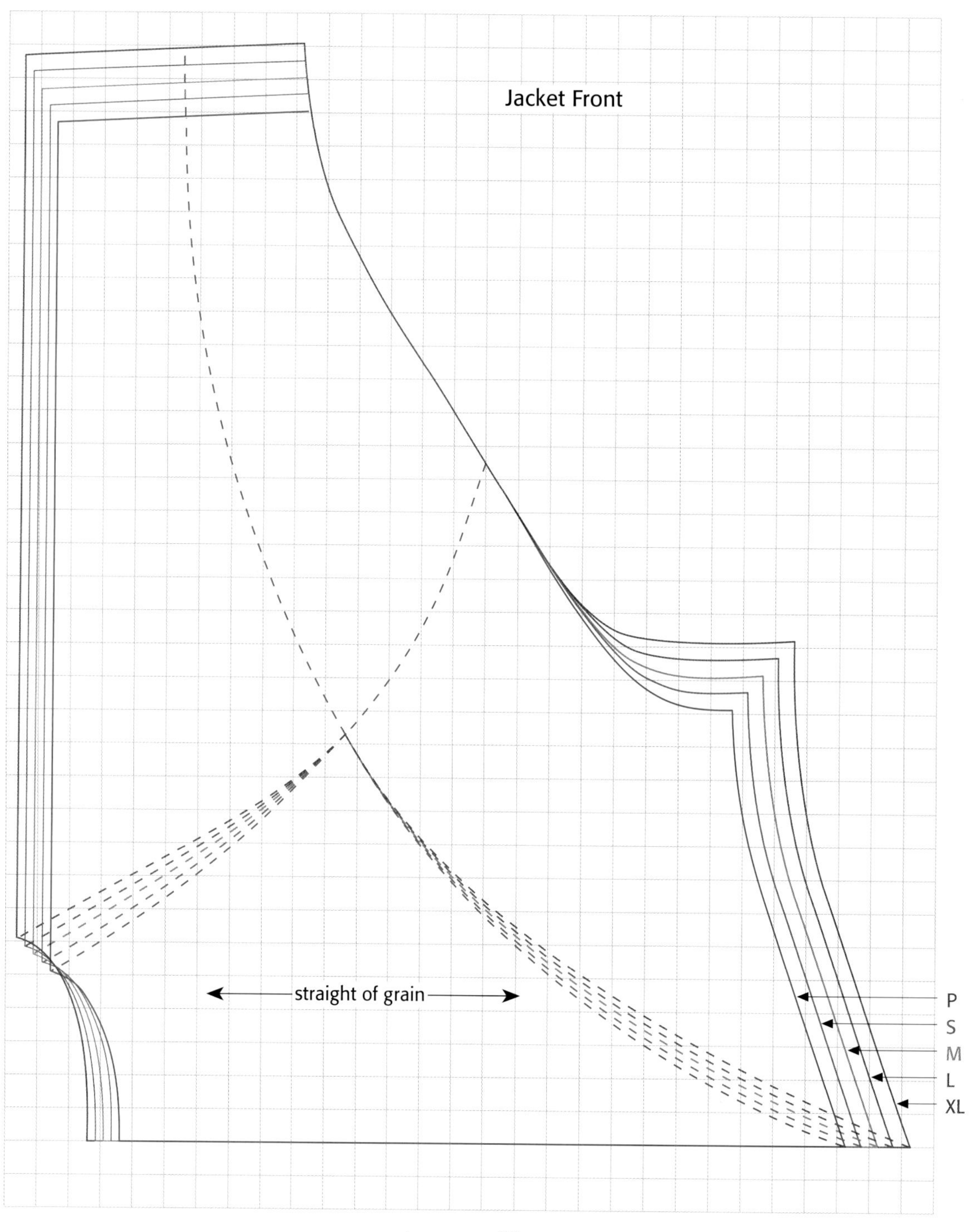

1 square = 1"

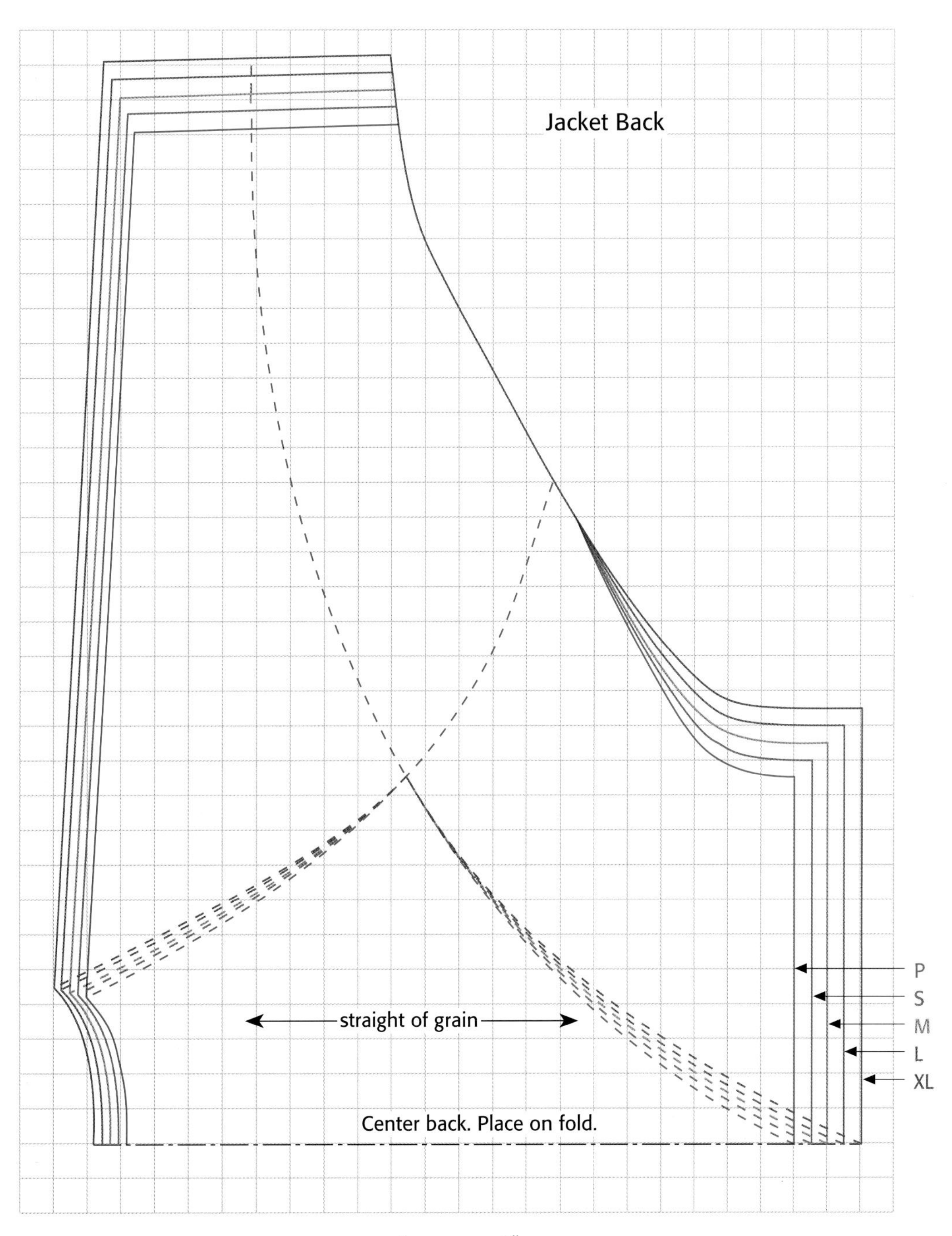
Jacket Back
straight of grain
P
S
M
L
XL
Center back. Place on fold.

1 square = 1"

Watermelon Medley Wall Hanging

I developed the colorations for this project during the construction of the watermelon handbag shown on page 71. The finished project looked so much like a watermelon that I was inspired to work on a series using this theme. I had visions of an entire kitchen decorated in watermelon chenille, including seat cushions, pillows, and rugs, with a wall hanging as the centerpiece. I hope you will have as much fun with this as I did.

Watermelon Medley Wall Hanging
by Nannette Holmberg, 43½" x 59".

Yardage Requirements

*45" wide, 100% cotton**

Note: Do not pre-shrink any of the fabrics for this project

10⅛ yd. natural colored muslin
⅝ yd. *each* medium and dark pink
¼ yd. *each* medium and dark green
½ yd. light green
¾ yd. black
45" x 61" piece of needlepunched cotton batting

*If you can't find muslin that is 45" wide, you may need to reposition the appliqués for a narrower fabric.

Supplies

Coordinating thread
Water-soluble gluestick or spray adhesive
Tailor's chalk or water-soluble marking pen

Cutting

1. From the muslin, cut the following pieces:
   2 base layers, each 45" x 61"
   3 chenille layers, each 43" x 59"
2. Referring to the dimensions on the quilt diagram, cut the medium pink and light green blocks.

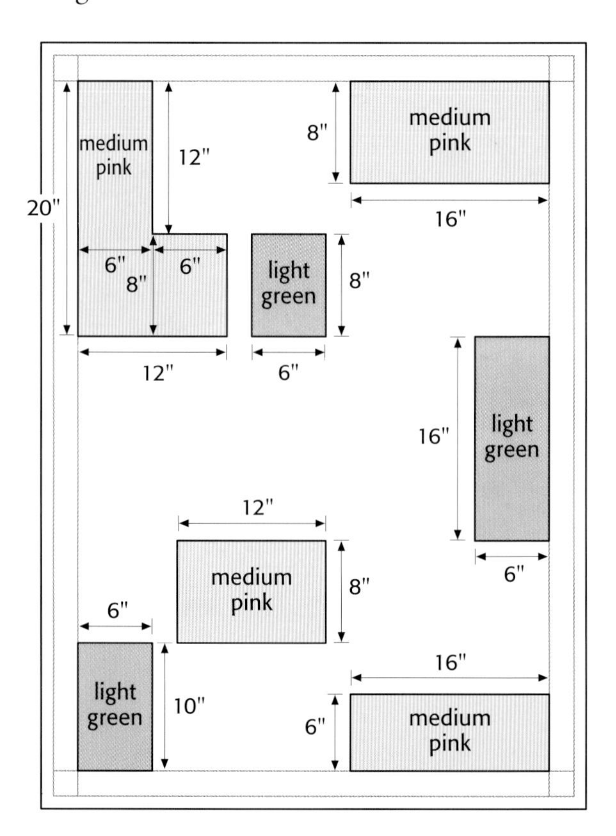

3. Cut and layer the dark pink fabric over the medium pink fabric, and the medium green over the dark green—the doubled fabric layers will give the appliqué colorations depth. Using the patterns on pages 68–69, prepare and cut the watermelon appliqués from the layered fabrics, taking care to position grain lines properly.
4. Cut the leaves from single layers of green fabric. Refer to the quilt diagram on page 66 to cut the leaves from the fabric with correct grain lines.
5. Cut 75 black squares and 74 muslin squares, each 2" x 2".
6. Cut ½"-wide bias strips from each of the greens to use for vines.

Chenille Assembly

1. Place 1 of the muslin base layers on a table, wrong side up. Place the needlepunched batting over the fabric, then lay the remaining base layer on top, right side up. Smooth out the layers. *Note:* You can use spray adhesive to hold these layers together.
2. Center the 3 chenille layers on top of the base layers, right sides up, allowing about 1" of the base layers to extend beyond the chenille layers all the way around. Pin the corners and outer edges.

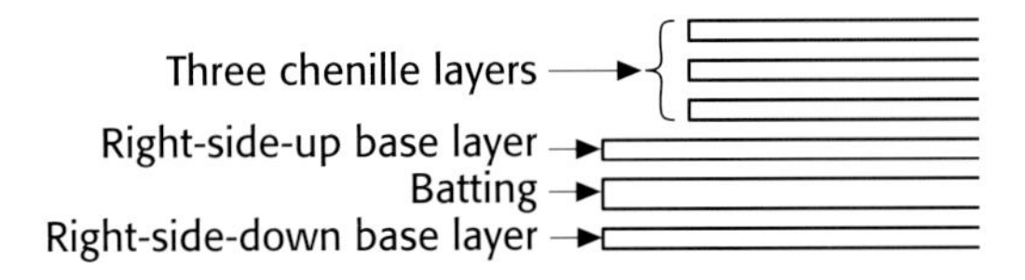

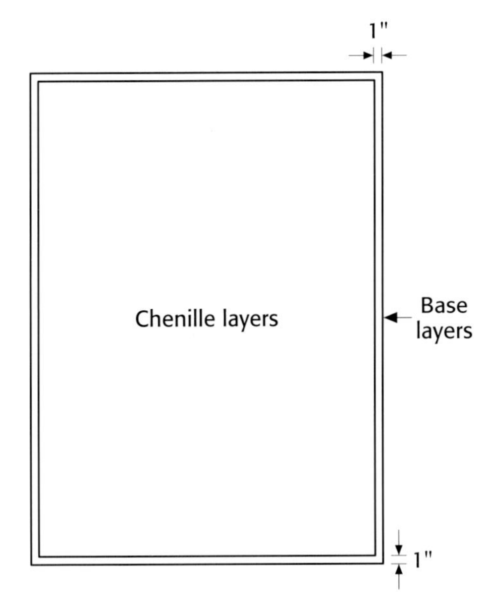

3. Using a washable chalk marker or water-soluble marking pen, draw a line 1" from each edge of the top chenille layer. Draw another line 2" inside the first.
4. Referring to the quilt diagram, draw placement lines. Marking guidelines on the surface of the quilt makes it easier to place design elements properly.
5. Place the black and cream squares on the quilt, securing them with spray adhesive. Once the squares are in place, randomly pin a few of them through all the layers to secure the layers for stitching.

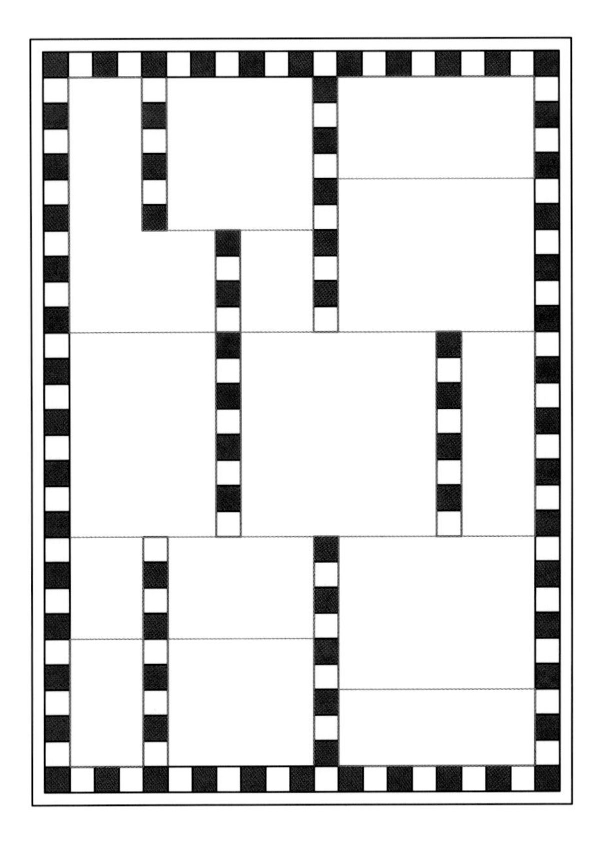

Tip: I find that on a large project like this, spray adhesive works better than gluestick or pins, holding shapes in place throughout the stitching process. Test your adhesive first to make sure it has sufficient holding power. Some adhesives do not hold well when fabrics are continually manipulated.

6. Place the light green and medium pink blocks on the quilt, securing them with adhesive spray.

7. Position the watermelon slices on the quilt, placing the medium pink piece first and the dark piece directly on top of it. Put the green rind shapes next to the watermelon sections, laying the light green piece first and the medium green piece on top.

8. Put the seeds on the watermelons. Notice that a few watermelon seeds are placed above the angled slice of watermelon at the lower edge of the wall hanging.

Tip: I spread all my seeds out on a sheet of butcher paper and sprayed them at one time with adhesive. It was easy to pick up and place each one on the watermelon slices.

9. Place the medium green whole watermelon at lower right and lay the light green shading strips on top. Place a dark green leaf at the left end of the watermelon.
10. Position the remaining leaves as shown in the diagram above. Using the ½"-wide bias strips, "twine" stems from each leaf, choosing various shades of green.
11. Check the surface of the quilt, making sure that it is pinned closely enough to hold everything in place while you quilt. Chalk-mark a 45° angle across the middle of the quilt to mark your first row of stitching.

12. Roll 1 section of your quilt and pin it out of the way.
13. Stitch along the line you marked in step 11. When you finish the row, turn the quilt and begin a second row, ⅜" from the stitching line. Do not make the channels any wider than ⅜".

Note: Be aware of the appliqué pieces as you stitch. Some may fall off or move out of position during stitching and handling. This is where the guidelines you drew in step 4 will be important, making it easy to reposition anything that comes loose.

Manipulating the quilt as little as possible helps to avoid this problem. Setting your machine on a large table—where your quilt will have room to lie undisturbed as you sew instead of falling to the floor—also helps to keep appliqués from falling off.

14. Continue stitching until you've covered half the quilt top, then stitch the other side.
15. Once the quilt is completely stitched, it's time to slash it. Slash every channel in the quilt, cutting through the appliqués and the top 3 fabric layers. Take care to leave the batting and the 2 base layers intact. Start at the edges and cut between the stitching lines, down the center of each channel, using scissors or strips and a rotary cutter. Leave the batting and the two base layers of fabric intact. (Refer to "Sample Blocks" on pages 34–35 for basic cutting directions.)

    Note: If you are using cutting strips, remember that your strips are not as long as the channels, and you must slide them along the channel as you cut. Do not run off the edge, or you may cut the base layers. If you do accidentally cut the base fabric, refer to "Mending Cuts and Holes" on page 38 for repair tips.

Finishing

1. Trim the edges ½" from the checkerboard border. Make sure each corner is a perfect 90° angle. A clear acrylic ruler and a rotary cutter will provide the cleanest and most accurate edges and corners.

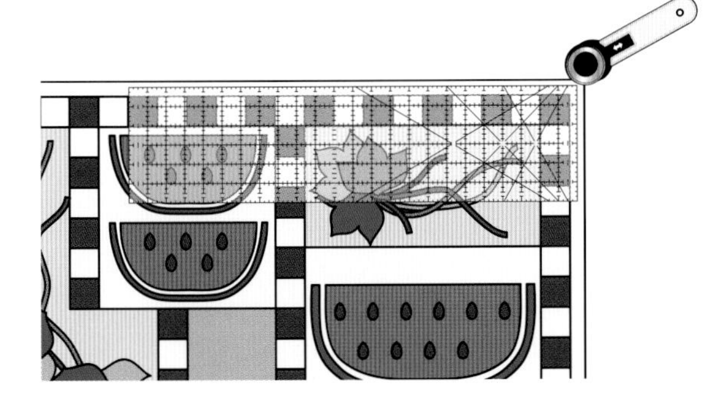

2. Refer to "Cutting and Applying Bias Binding Strips" on pages 39–40 to cut 2¼"-wide bias strips from the black fabric. Join the strips end to end until you have a strip long enough to go around the perimeter of the quilt plus 15". Stitch the binding to the quilt, mitering the corners. Edgestitch the binding along the turned-under edge and close to the quilt outer edges.

    Note: I know it's not usually done on quilts, but I like to topstitch and edgestitch my bindings. Edgestitched binding seems to survive the chenille laundering process better than traditional binding. I have seen traditional binding on chenille garments and wall hangings come out of the washing process looking wrinkled and untidy. Edgestitched binding stays straight and neat.

    If you're not sure what kind of binding to use, make a sample block of your fabrics and bind the edges with both traditional and edgestitched binding. Put the block through the washing process and see which binding you prefer.

3. Wash the quilt using cold-water detergent and a regular machine cycle. Set the dryer at the permanent-press setting and dry the quilt completely.

Watermelon Variations

Use individual elements from the quilt to complete your watermelon ensemble. A checkered border surrounds one of the larger motifs for a simply scrumptious rug, while two of the smaller motifs work perfectly to create a panel for the Four-Seasons pillow (instructions begin on page 77).

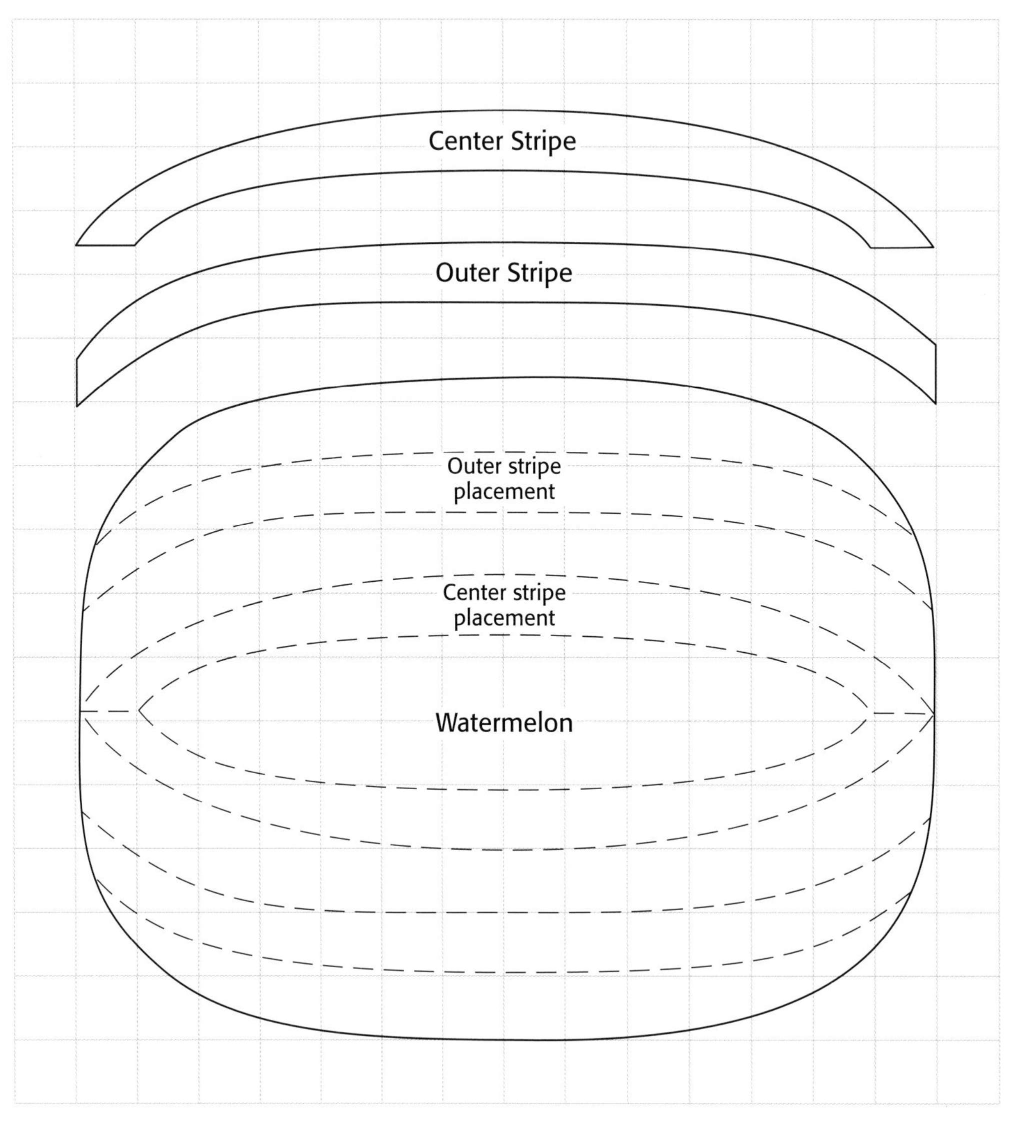
Center Stripe
Outer Stripe
Outer stripe placement
Center stripe placement
Watermelon

1 square = 1"

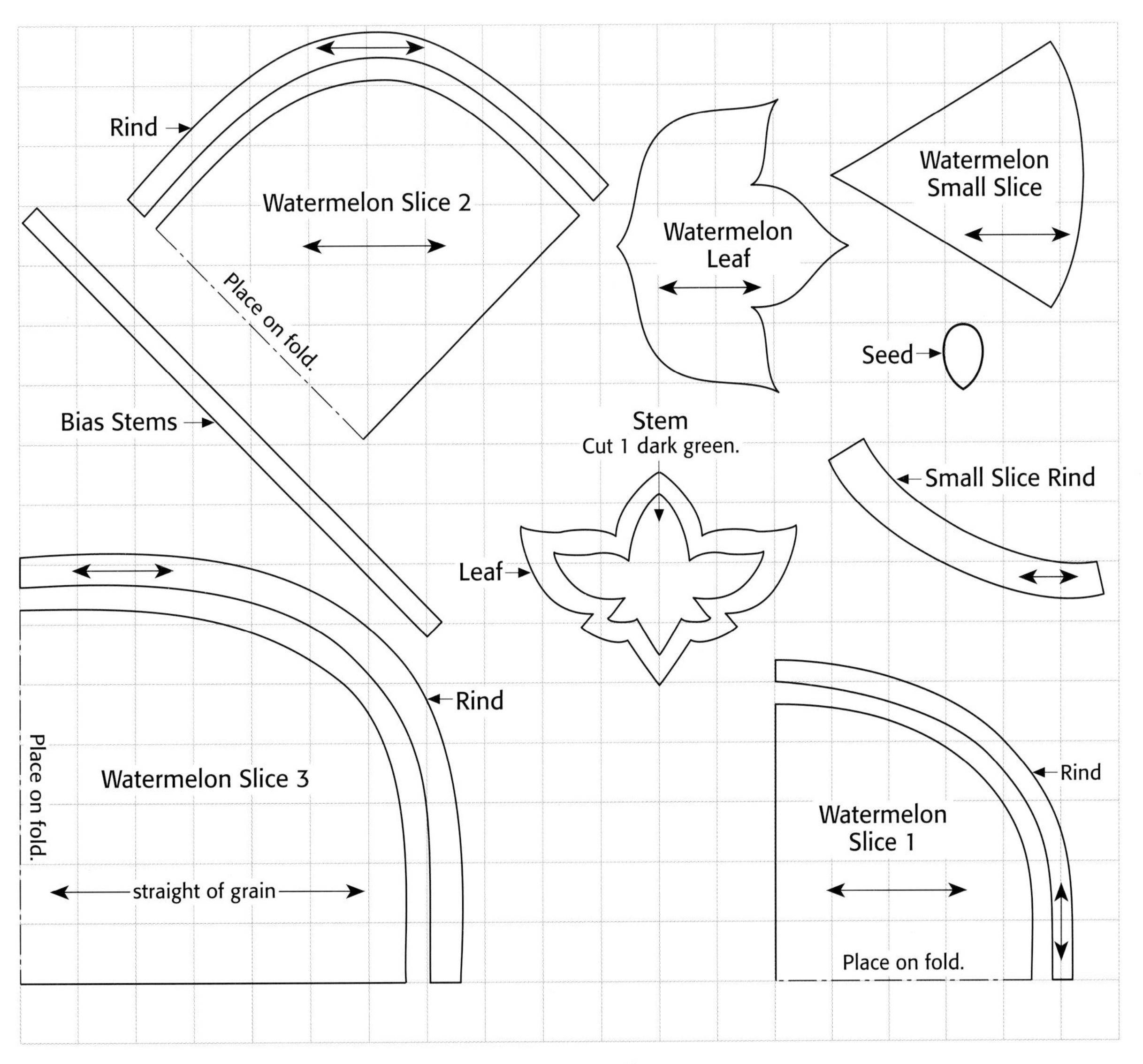
Rind
Watermelon Slice 2
Place on fold.
Bias Stems
Watermelon Leaf
Watermelon Small Slice
Seed
Stem
Cut 1 dark green.
Small Slice Rind
Leaf
Rind
Place on fold.
Watermelon Slice 3
straight of grain
Rind
Watermelon Slice 1
Place on fold.

1 square = 1"

Watermelon Handbag

This slice of summer can also be a great pillow. Just sew the top shut instead of adding a zipper, and eliminate the straps.

Yardage Requirements

44"-wide, 100% cotton

Note: Do not pre-shrink any of the fabrics for this project.

½ yd. dark red
½ yd. medium red
1⅛ yds. light red
½ yd. light pink heavyweight cotton
⅜ yd. cream
⅛ yd. black
1 yd. light green
1 yd. dark green
1 yd. for lining
2 strips, each 2½" x 32", of cotton needle-punched batting

Supplies

Cream thread
20"-long cream zipper
Water-soluble gluestick or spray adhesive
Tailor's chalk or water-soluble marking pen

Assembly

1. Following the directions on page 41, prepare the pattern pieces.
2. Layer the dark, medium, and light red fabrics as shown. Cut 2 watermelon sections and 1 strip, 5" x 22".

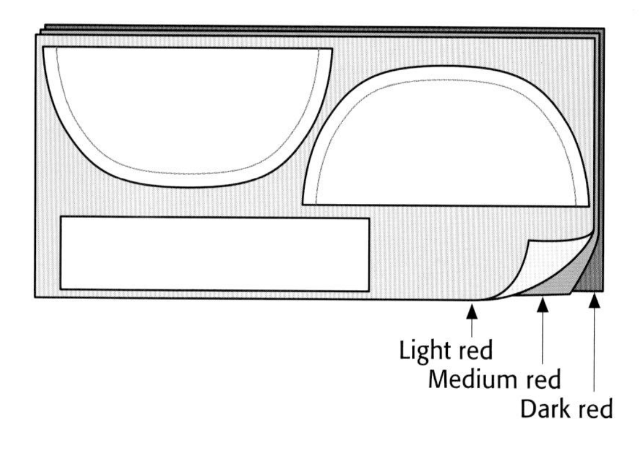

3. Place the lining fabric right side down, then lay the light pink heavyweight cotton over it, right side up. Place the layered watermelon sections and the 5" x 22" strip on top of the layered fabrics, right side up. Cut around each piece, 1" from the edges. Pin the strip layers together and then set them aside.

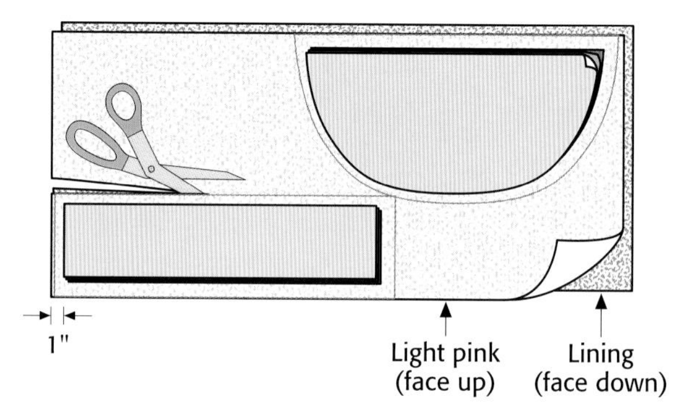

4. Cut 2 edge strips from the cream fabric; place 1 strip along each curved edge of the watermelon sections. Use adhesive spray to secure the strips.

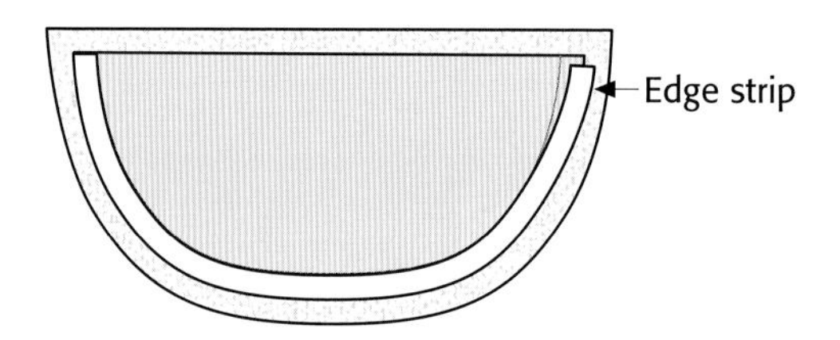

5. Using the pattern you made in step 1, cut 30 black seeds. Place 15 seeds in 3 rows on each watermelon. Use gluestick or adhesive spray to hold the seeds in place.
6. Pin the edges of each watermelon in place. If necessary, pin each seed to secure.

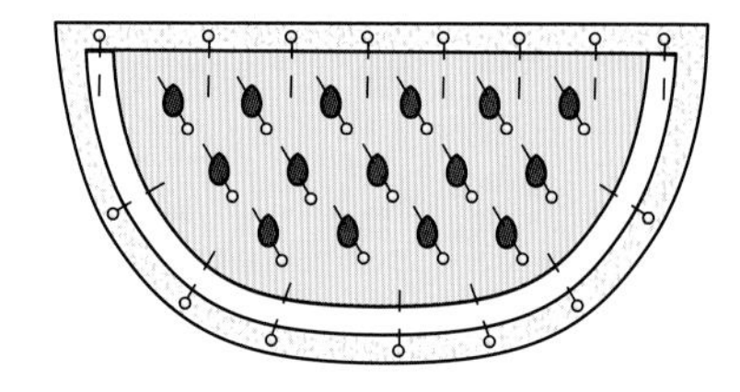

7. Chalk-mark a vertical line down the center of each watermelon section. Draw a 45° angle from each side of the center vertical line. Stitch along this line, pivoting at the center, then continue stitching parallel rows ⅜" apart until the entire watermelon section is quilted.

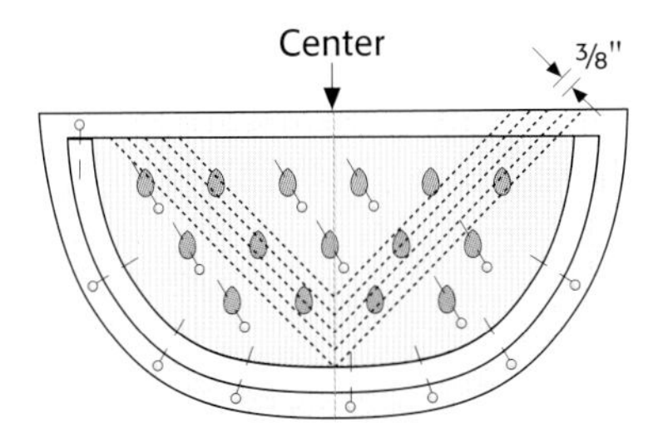

8. Taking care not to cut the heavyweight pink fabric and lining layers, slash the top 3 layers and the seed appliqués. Cut between the stitching lines, down the center of each channel, using scissors or a rotary cutter and strips (refer to "Sample Blocks" on pages 34–35 for basic cutting directions).
9. When you are done slashing, place the paper pattern over the slashed layers and trim the excess.

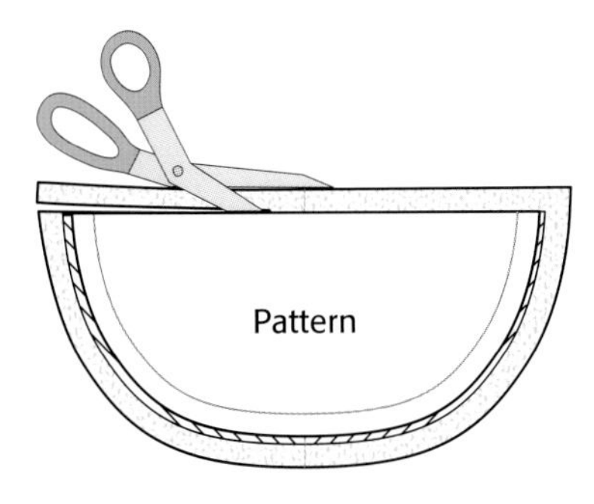

10. Fold the light green fabric in half vertically, and cut along the fold.
11. Fold the dark green fabric in half vertically to make 2 layers. Layer 1 light green piece over the 2 dark green layers. Cut 1 rind section from the layered fabrics.

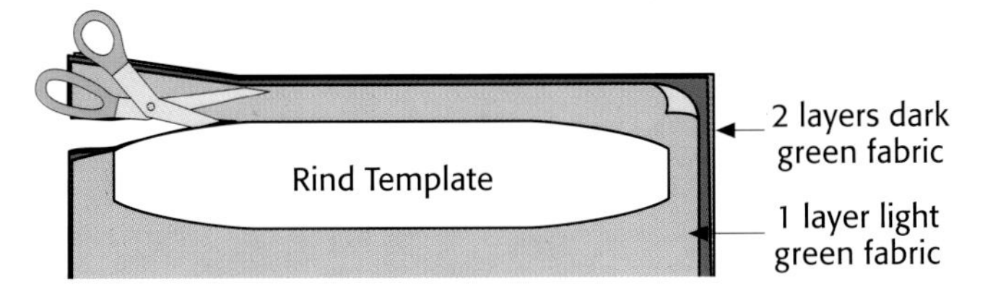

12. Place the remaining lining fabric right side down, and layer 1 light green piece over it, right side up. Place the layered rind section on top. Cut the lining layers 1" from the edges of the rind section. Pin randomly around the edges to secure.

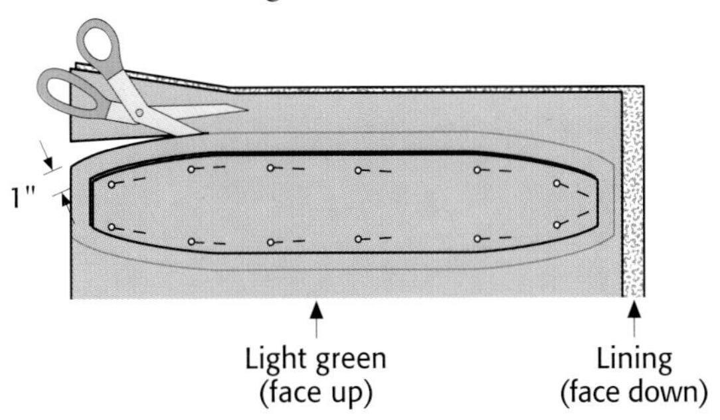

13. Chalk-mark a line at a 45°-angle to intersect the middle of the rind section. Stitch along this line, then continue stitching parallel rows ⅜" apart until the entire piece is quilted.

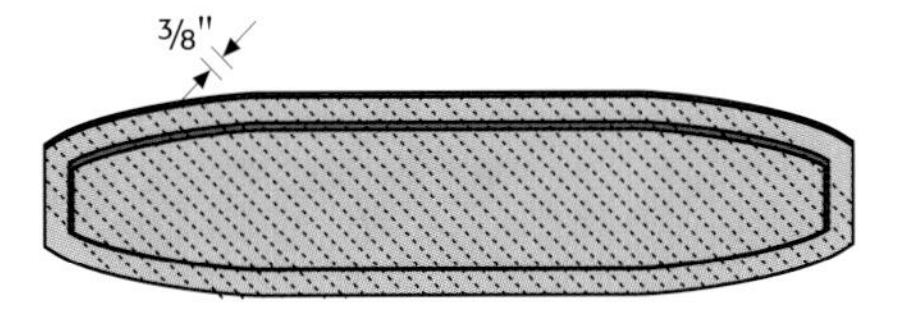

14. Taking care not to cut the light green layer and lining, slash the 3 chenille layers between the rows of stitching. When you are done slashing, place the paper pattern over the slashed layers and trim the excess.
15. Chalk-mark a 45° angle line across the 5" x 22" layered strip. Stitch along this line, then continue stitching parallel rows ⅜" apart until the entire section is quilted. Taking care not to cut the heavyweight pink fabric and lining layers, slash the top 3 layers. Cut between the stitching lines, down the center of each channel, using scissors or a rotary cutter and strips.
16. Cut the layered strip in half lengthwise to yield 2 pieces, each 1½" x 21".

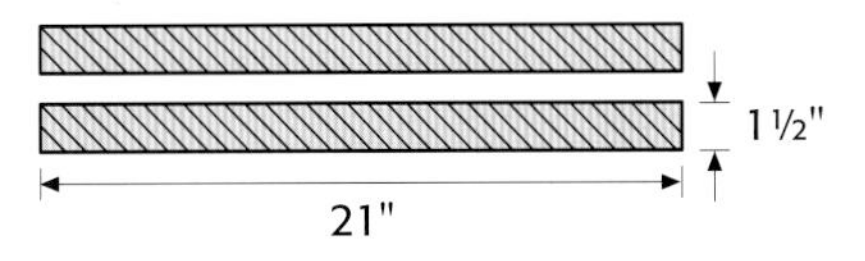

17. Referring to "Cutting and Applying Bias Binding Strips" on pages 39–40, from the light red fabric, cut 2 bias strips, each 1¼" x 22". With the strips, bind 1 long edge of each 1½" x 21" strip you cut in step 16, using a ¼"-wide seam allowance.

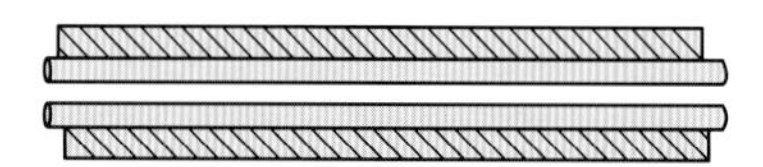

18. With the zipper right side up, place the bound edge of one 21"-long strip along one side of the zipper, allowing ½" extra at the end of each strip. Pin every few inches. With a zipper foot on your sewing machine, stitch close to the edge of the binding, next to the zipper teeth. Repeat with the remaining bound strip on the other side of the zipper.

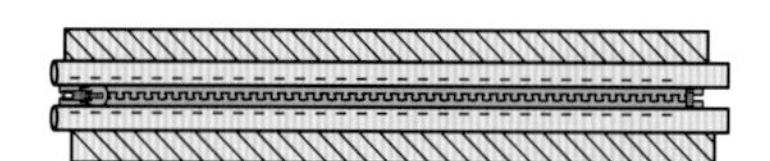

19. With wrong (lining) sides together, pin the watermelon sections to the rind section, then stitch with a ¼"-wide seam allowance.

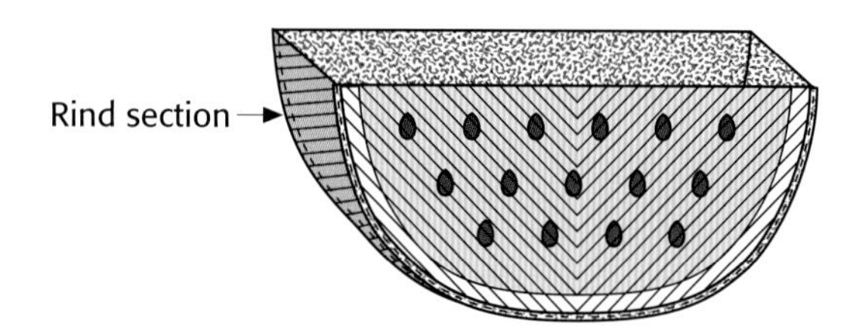

20. Cut 1¼"-wide bias strips from green fabric and join them end to end as needed to make 2 strips, each 31½" long. Bind the watermelon/rind seams.

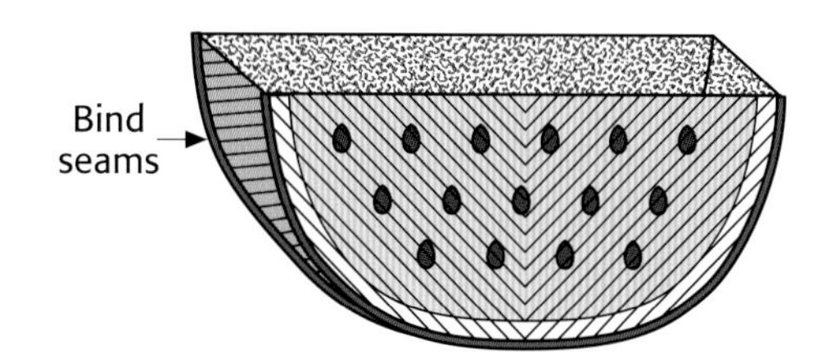

21. With wrong (lining) sides together, pin the zipper section to the tops and ends of the watermelon section, then stitch with a ¼"-wide seam allowance.

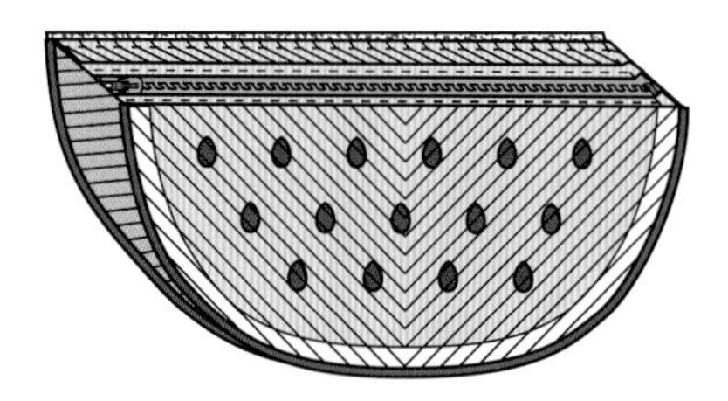

22. Cut 1½"-wide bias strips from the light red fabric and join them end to end as needed to make a 50"-long strip. Bind the seams at the top of the bag, mitering the corners. Edgestitch the binding along the turned-under edge and close to the outer edges.

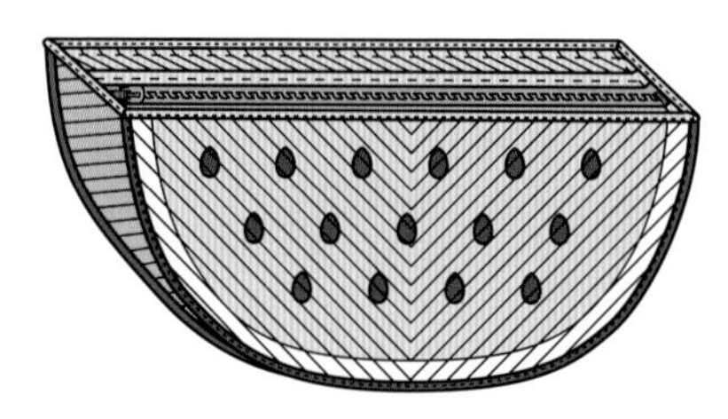

23. For the straps, cut 2 strips, each 2½" x 32", from the light red fabric. Place a strip, right side up, on each needlepunched batting strip and baste in place.

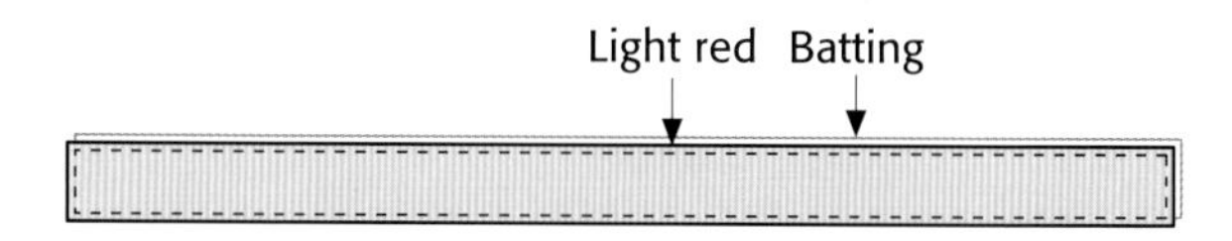

24. Fold the strips in half lengthwise with right sides together. Stitch along the long raw edge of each strip with a ¼"-wide seam allowance. Turn and press, centering the seam at the back of each strap. Topstitch ⅛" and ⅜" from each edge.

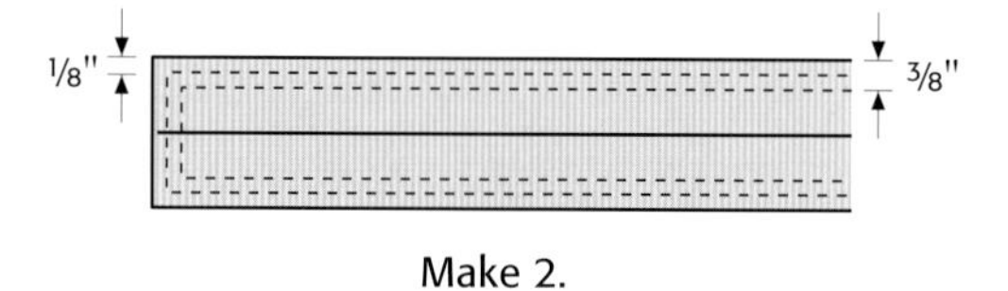

Make 2.

25. Fold the ends of each strap under 1". Pin the straps to the bag and stitch the ends in place as shown.

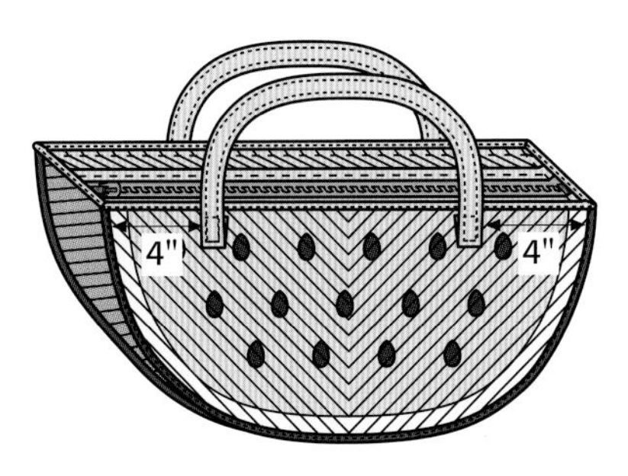

26. Wash the bag on a regular setting. Set the dryer at "permanent press" and dry the bag completely.

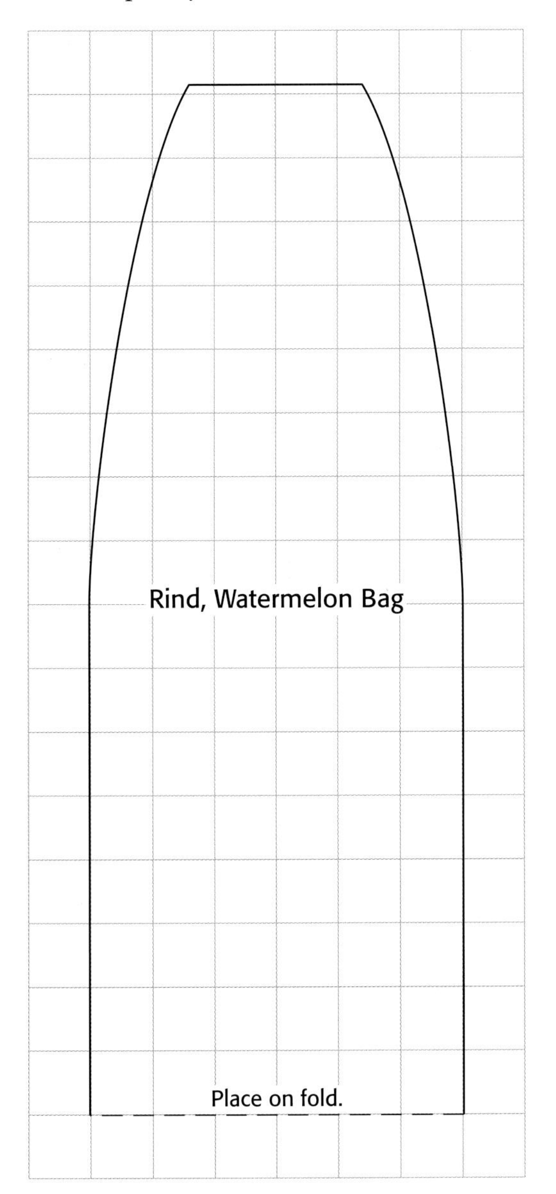

1 square = 1"

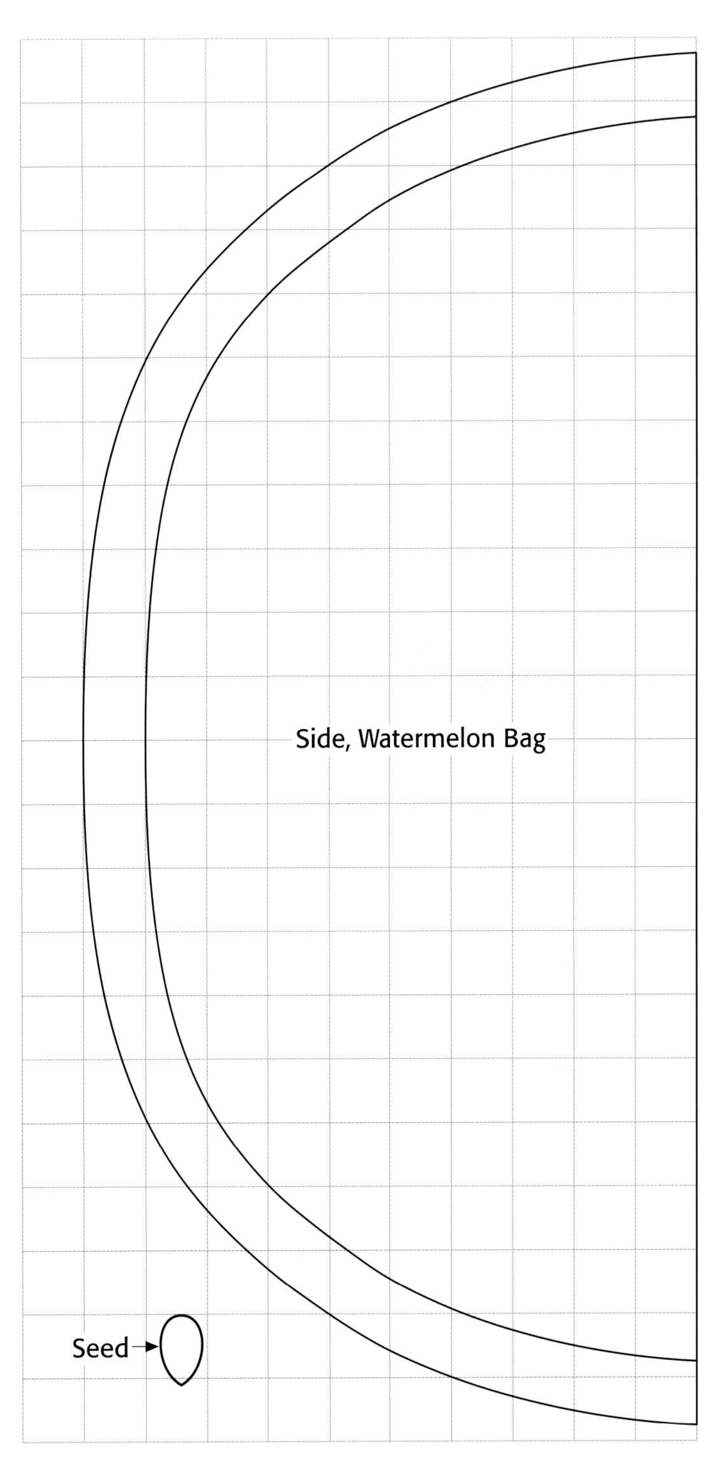

1 square = 1"

Four-Seasons Pillow

I got the idea for this pillow while traveling in Europe. A small shop in Germany had pillows with beautifully embroidered panels that tied onto buttons. I thought the pillows were charming and loved the notion of changing designs on pillows to give a room a new look. When I tried the panel technique in chenille, the result was a single pillow I could transform to fit the season.

Yardage Requirements

44"-wide, 100% cotton

5 yds. muslin for pillowcase, 4 chenille panels, bias binding, and ties*
Winter trees: two 8" x 9" pieces, 1 green and 1 burgundy
Spring leaves: one 6" x 12" piece *each* of light, medium, and dark green; one 6" x 6" square *each* of purple, red, and yellow
Summer petals: one 5" x 5" square of brown, and one 10" x 10" square *each* of yellow and gold
Autumn leaves: one 12" x 12" square of variegated red

**Be sure to cut the chenille pieces before prewashing the remaining fabric.*

Supplies

16"-long nylon coil zipper
Cream thread
4 buttons, 5/8" diameter
Water-soluble gluestick or spray adhesive
Tailor's chalk or water-soluble marking pen
18" x 18" pillow form

Chenille Panel Cutting

From unwashed muslin, cut the following pieces:

4 squares, each 16" x 16", for base layers

12 squares, each 14" x 14", for chenille layers

Bias strips to total 1¾" x 216", for binding; join end to end as needed (refer to "Cutting and Applying Bias Binding Strips" on pages 39–40)

16 bias strips, each 1¼" x 15", for ties

Pillow

1. After cutting the chenille panel pieces, wash and dry the remaining muslin.
2. From the prewashed muslin, cut the following pieces:

   1 square, 17½" x 17½"
   2 rectangles, each 9⅜" x 17½", for back panels
   8 bands, each 3" x 23¾"; cut each end at opposite 45° angles

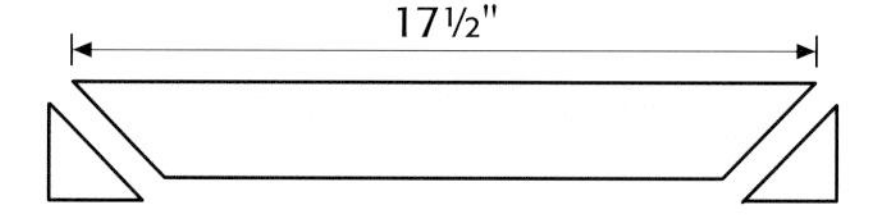

3. Press under 5/8" along one 17½" edge of each back panel.

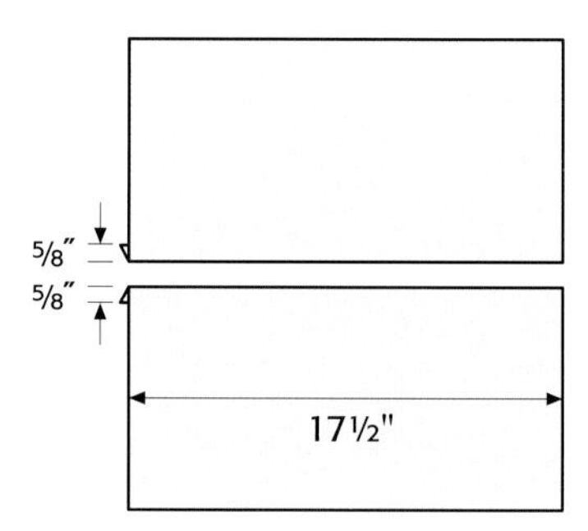

4. Pin the folded edge of one panel close to the zipper coil on one side, and stitch. Lap the folded edge of the remaining panel over the zipper coil until it barely covers the first stitching line. Pin along the folded edge as shown. Stitch close to the coil on the unstitched side of the zipper tape.

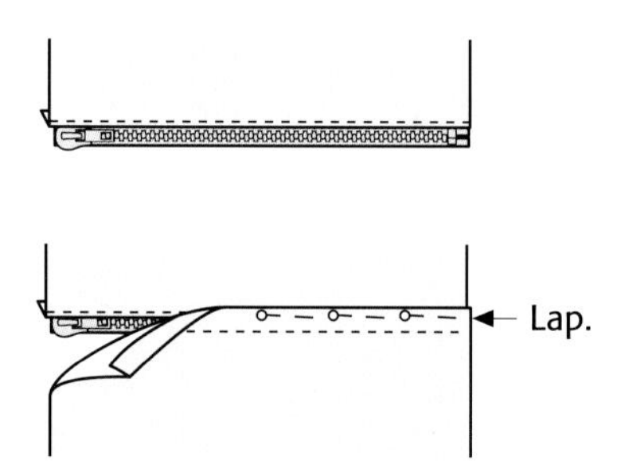

5. Using a ¼"-wide seam allowance, sew 4 band sections together at the corners to form an open frame. Stitch from the outer corner to ¼" from the inner edge, and backstitch. Sew the second set of band sections together in the same manner.

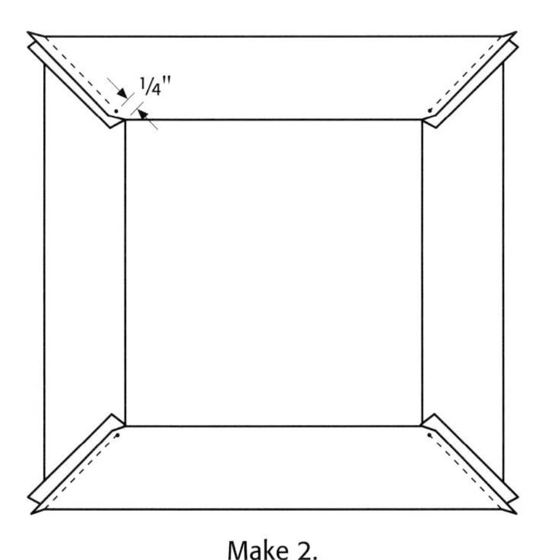

Make 2.

6. With right sides together, sew one frame to the pillow top, matching the inner edge of the frame to the edge of the pillow, and pivoting at the corners. Press the seam allowances toward the frame.

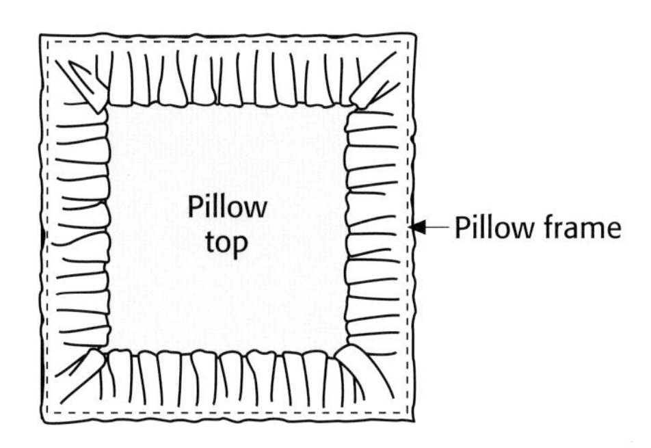

7. With the zipper closed, sew the second frame to the pillow back, pinning the lapped edge to keep it from gapping. Press the seam allowances toward the frame.

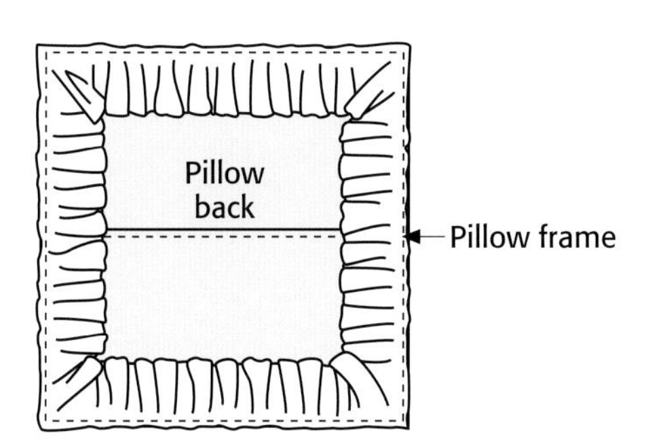

8. Open the zipper halfway. Place the pillow front and back right sides together, and stitch along the edges with a ¼"-wide seam allowance, pivoting at the corners. Trim the corners, then turn the pillowcase right side out through the zipper opening.

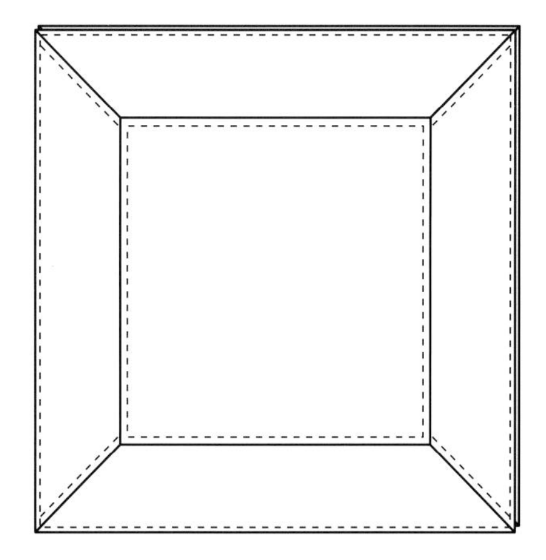

9. With the top of the pillow facing up, stitch in the ditch of the seam that joins the frame to the pillow.

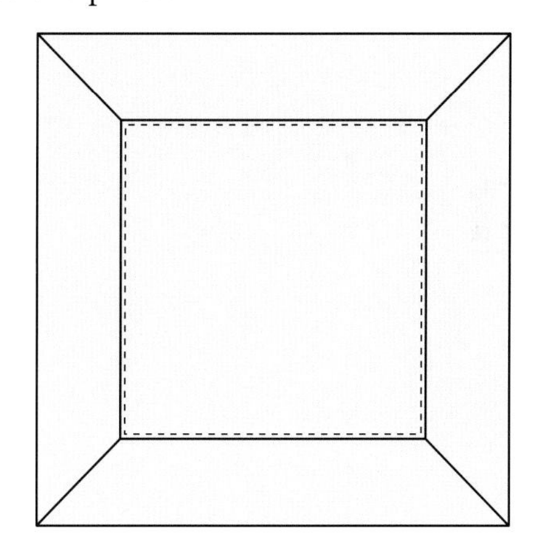

10. Sew a button to each corner of the pillow top as shown.

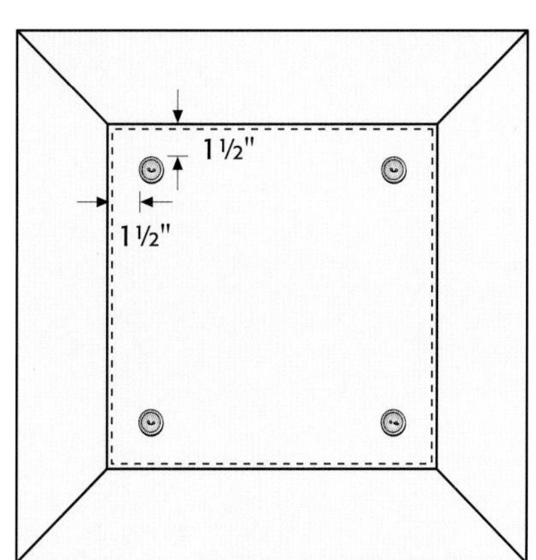

Panels

1. Stack three 14" muslin squares on top of each 16" base layer, with a 1" margin around all 4 edges of the stack. Pin the edges together.

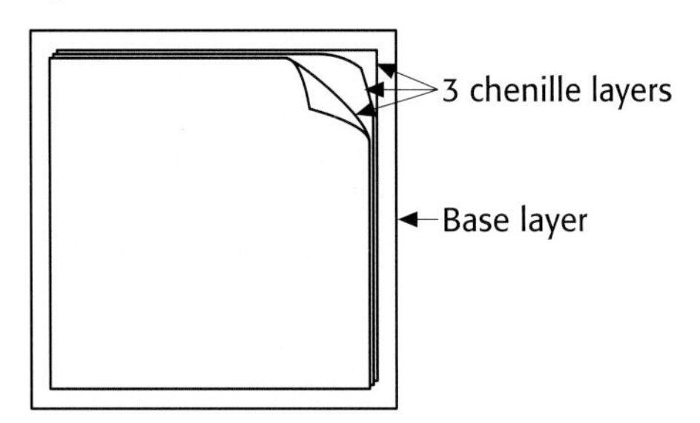

2. Prepare the patterns on pages 81–83 (see "Preparing the Pattern" on page 41). Cut the motifs from the appropriate fabrics. Remember to cut appliqués so that the straight of grain aligns with the muslin stack. Apply gluestick or temporary spray adhesive to the back of each appliqué shape, then position the appliqués on top of each stack, referring to the photos for placement. Pin randomly to hold the stack in place.

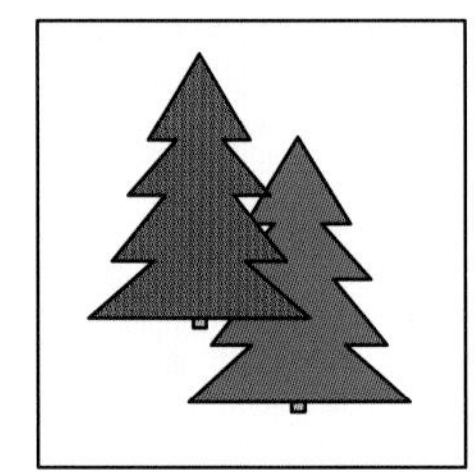

3. For the Spring, Fall, and Winter panels, use the washable chalk marker to draw a 45°-angle line across the center of the panel. Stitch along this line, then continue stitching parallel rows ⅜" apart until the entire panel is quilted.

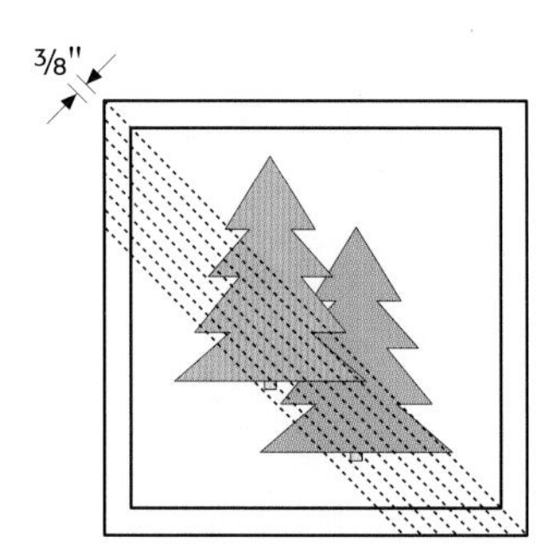

4. For the Summer panel, chalk-mark a line through the vertical and horizontal centers of the panel. Mark a line 45° from each center line as shown. Stitch along each line, then continue stitching parallel rows ⅜" apart until the entire section is quilted.

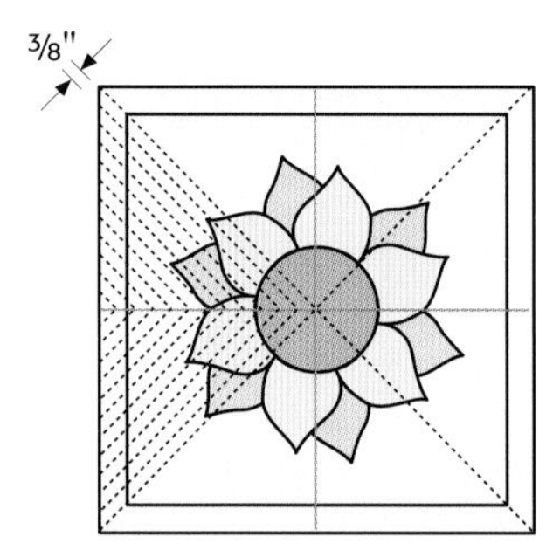

5. Taking care not to cut the bottom base layer, slash the top 3 layers and the appliqués on each panel. Cut between the stitching lines, down the center of each channel, using scissors or a rotary cutter and strips (refer to "Sample Blocks" on pages 34–35 for basic cutting instructions). Trim each panel to measure 13" x 13".
6. Referring to "Cutting and Applying Bias Binding Strips" on pages 39–40, bind the panel edges, using a ⅜"-wide seam allowance.

7. With right sides together, fold the tie strips together lengthwise and stitch with a scant ¼"-wide seam *from the folded edge.* Trim the cut edge to ¼". Turn. Do not press. Make 4 ties for each pillow.

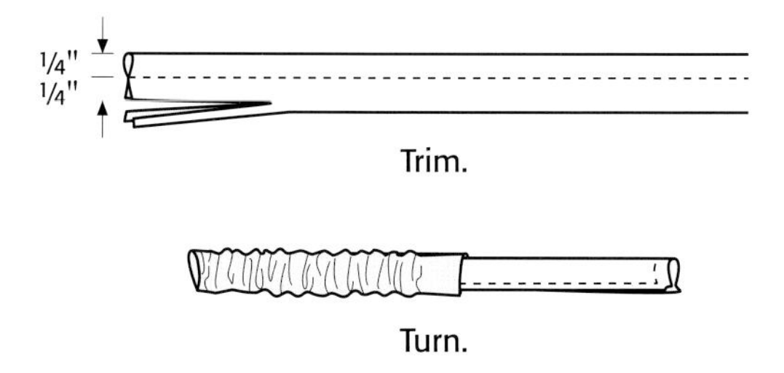

8. Fold each tie section in half. Place each folded end under a corner of the pillow panel. Stitch in place with 1 or 2 short, straight rows of stitching across the panel corner. Tie the panel onto the pillow top.

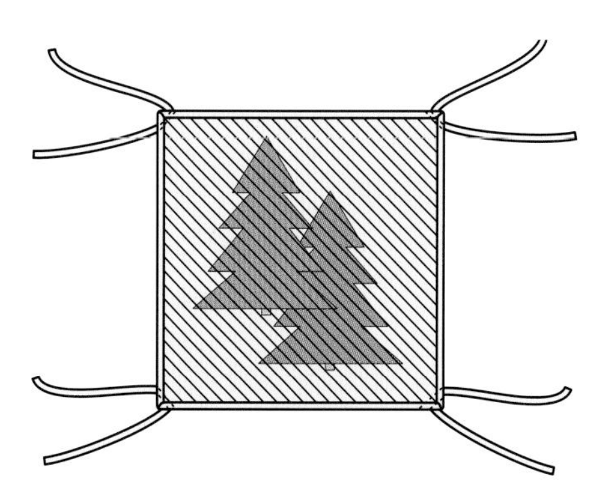

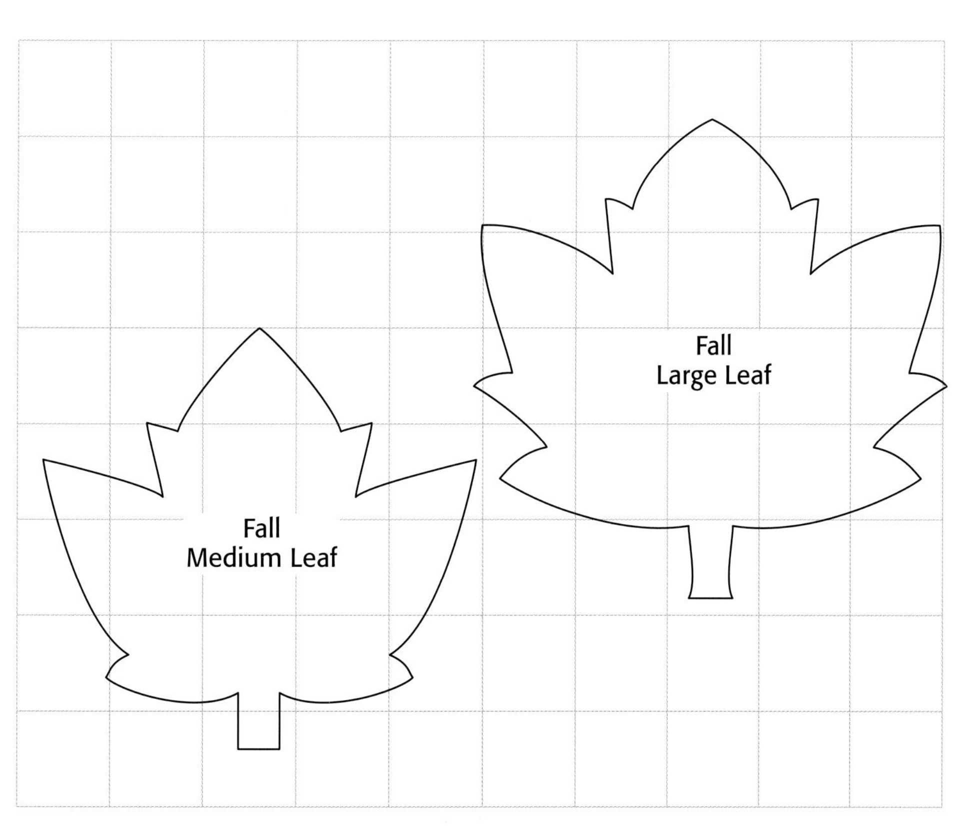

1 square = 1"

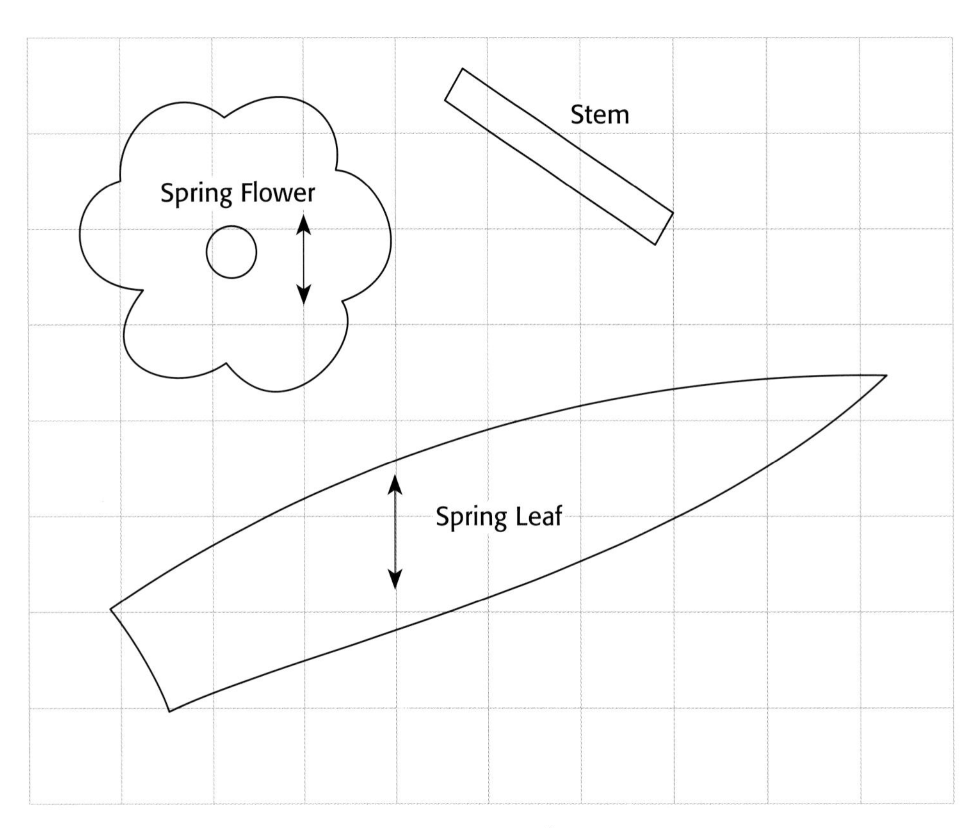

1 square = 1"

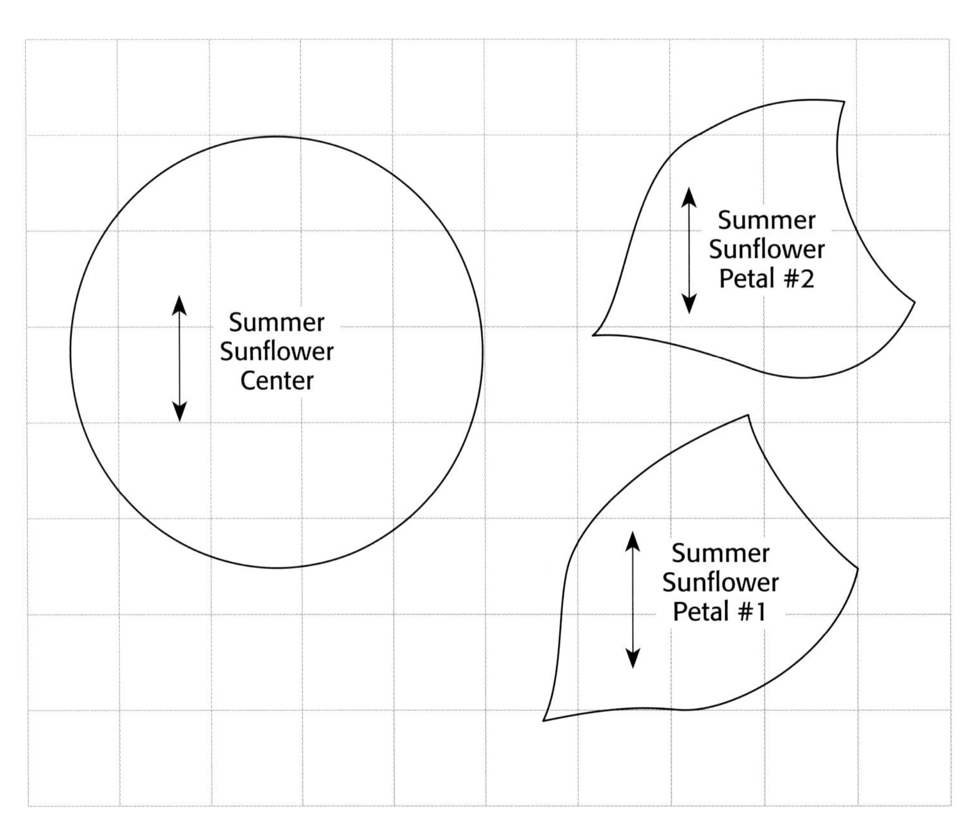

1 square = 1"

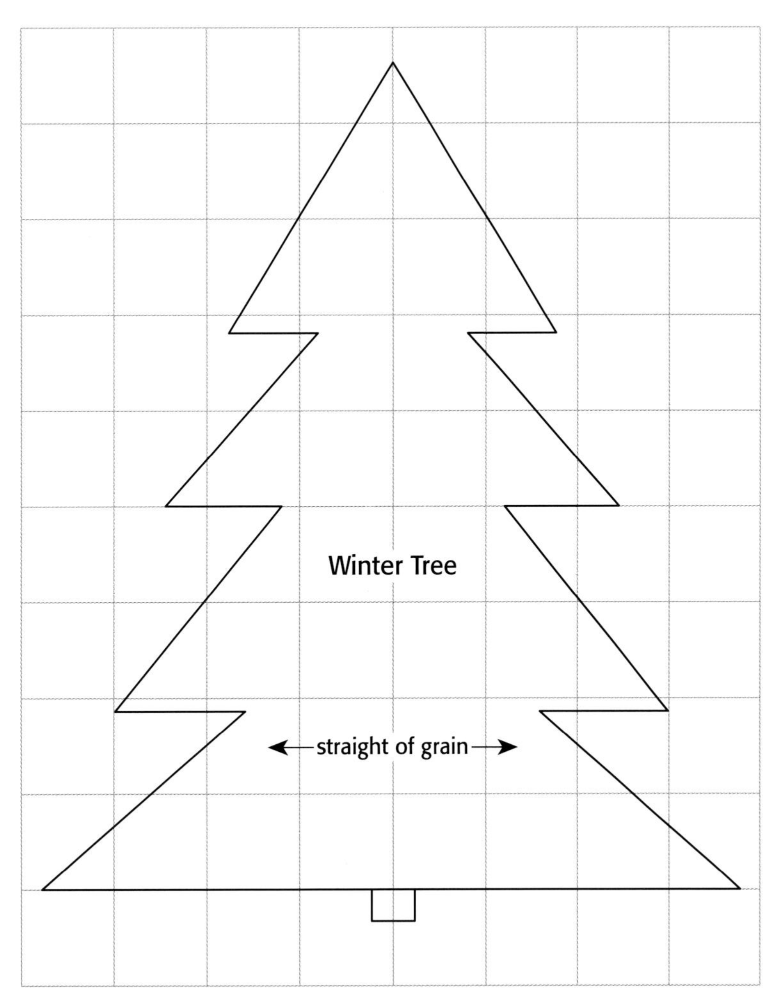

1 square = 1"

Twill-Weave Pillow

Weaving has become one of my favorite chenille techniques. With each new weaving design I learn, I find new ways to add interest to the surface of my chenille. Each pattern can be adapted to wearables as well as quilts and wall hangings. The basic design of this pillow will teach how to weave a twill pattern. Once you have mastered the repeats be sure to try the design in a jacket or vest.

Yardage Requirements

44"-wide, 100% cotton

23" x 23" square of light-colored cotton for pillow base layer
22" x 22" square of light-colored cotton for chenille base layer
20" x 20" square *each* of 1 dark-color and 1 light-color cotton
⅓ yd. of dark-color cotton for piping
2 rectangles, each 18½" x 22", for pillow-back sections

Supplies

2½ yds. of ¼"-wide cotton cording
Thread to match light-colored cotton
Water-soluble gluestick or spray adhesive
Tailor's chalk or water-soluble marking pen
18" x 18" pillow form

Assembly

1. Stack the 20" x 20" light square on top of the dark square. Draw a line down the left side, ½" from the edge. Using the tailor's chalk or marking pen, draw lines 1" apart across the square from bottom edge to top edge. Cut along these lines through both layers, ending at the ½" line on the left side of the squares.

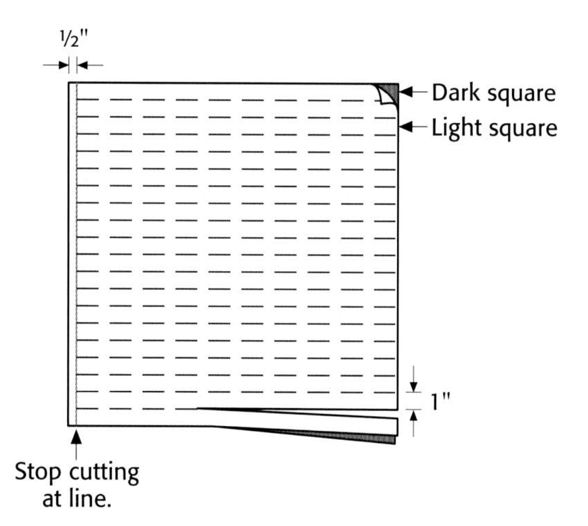

2. Apply gluestick or adhesive spray in a ½"-wide strip across the bottom edge of the 24" x 24" base square. Press the uncut edge of the light-colored cut square into place along the glued edge, starting ¾" from the right side of the square as shown. Pin along the bottom edge, then fold the strips back, away from the square. These strips will be the warp.

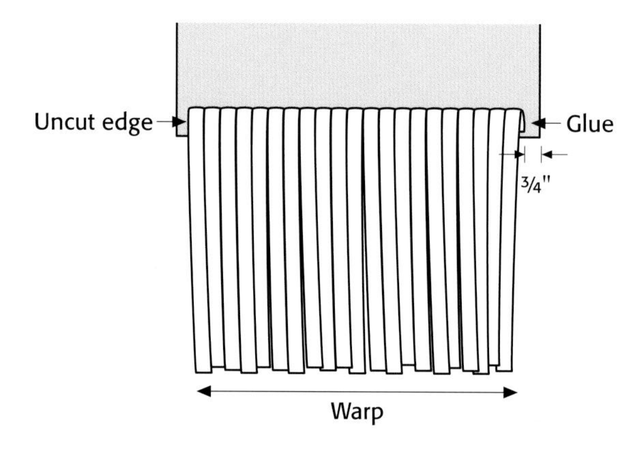

3. Apply gluestick or adhesive spray in a ½"-wide strip down the right side of the base square. Press the uncut edge of the dark-colored cut square into place along the glued edge, starting ¾" from the bottom of the square as shown. Pin along the right edge, then fold the strips back from the square. These strips will be the weft.

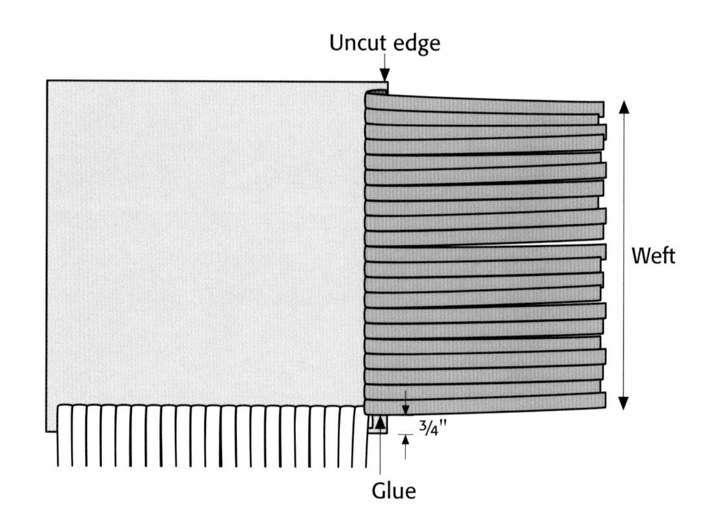

4. Fold the warp (light-colored) strips back into position on the chenille base. Pin the top edges to the base square.

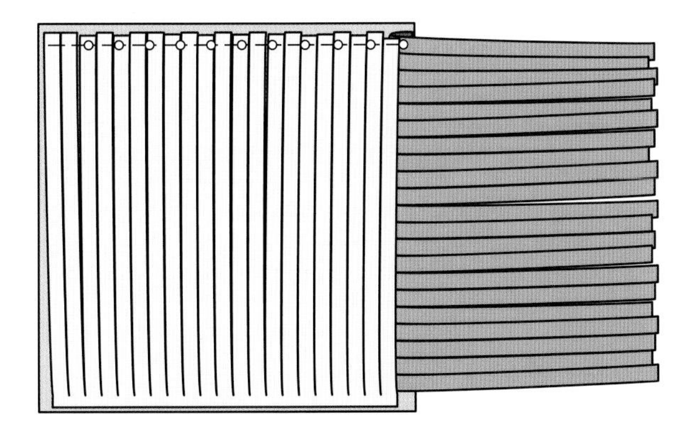

5. Insert a safety pin into the end of the lowest dark strip. The weaving-pattern repeat will be 4 strips wide and 4 rows deep—or a square, 4" x 4". The dark squares in the design represent where the dark weft strips cross over the warp. The light squares show where the dark weft strips cross under the warp. The squares are numbered 1, 2, 3, and 4, from right to left, repeating to the end of the row. Each row is numbered the same.
6. Starting at the bottom of the square, weave the first weft strip over 1 and 2, and under 3 and 4. Repeat this sequence to the end of the row. Pin the left edge in place as you finish each row. Attaching a large safety pin to the end of each strip as you weave it across the warp makes the "over-and-under moves" much easier.

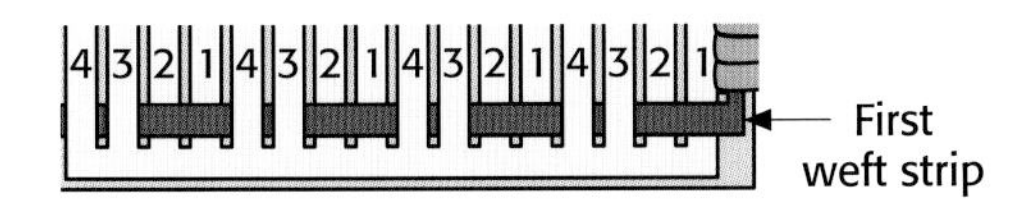

7. Weave the second strip under 1, over 2 and 3, and under 4. Repeat the pattern to the end of the row.

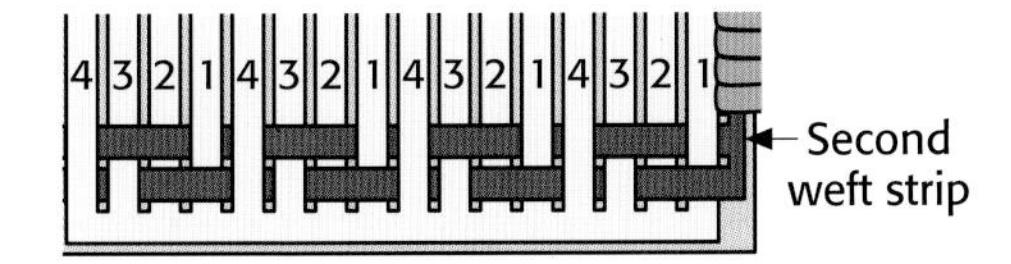

8. Weave the third strip under 1 and 2, and over 3 and 4. Repeat to the end of the row.

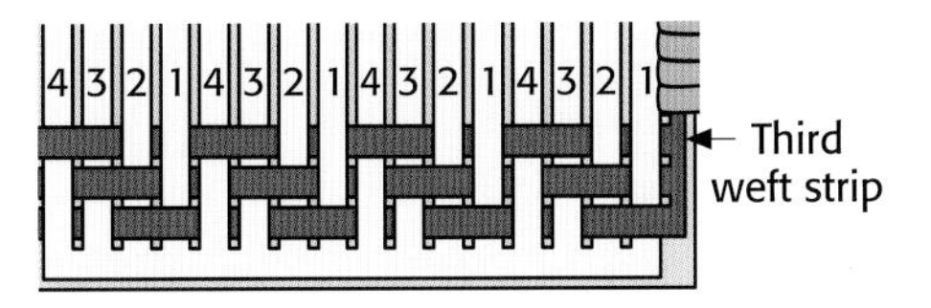

9. Weave the fourth strip over 1, under 2 and 3, and over 4. Repeat to the end of the row.

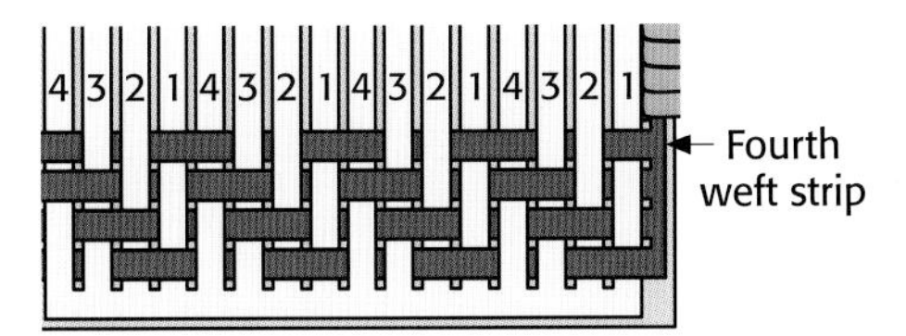

10. Repeat the 4-row sequence in steps 7–10 until the pillow top is completely woven.
11. Lay the woven layers on the 23" x 23" base layer, leaving ½" showing on all 4 sides.

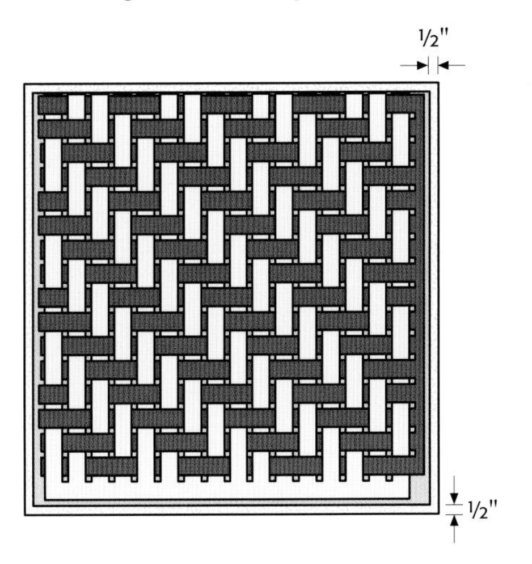

12. Draw a 45° angle across the center of pillow to mark the first row of stitching. Pin randomly over the surface. Stitch along this line, then continue stitching parallel rows ⅜" apart until the entire surface is quilted.

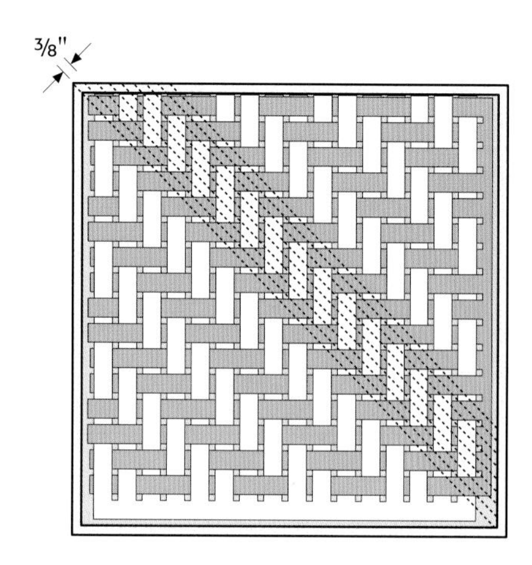

13. Slash down the center between each row of stitching, cutting all the layers except the base layer (refer to "Sample Blocks" on pages 34–35 for basic cutting directions).
14. Wash the chenille square in a washer on the regular setting. Set the dryer at permanent-press and dry completely.
15. Trim the square to 18½" x 18½".
16. Fold the pillow-back sections in half to measure 11" x 18½" each. Press. Overlap the folded edges of each section until they form a perfect 18½" square. Pin the sides together where they overlap.

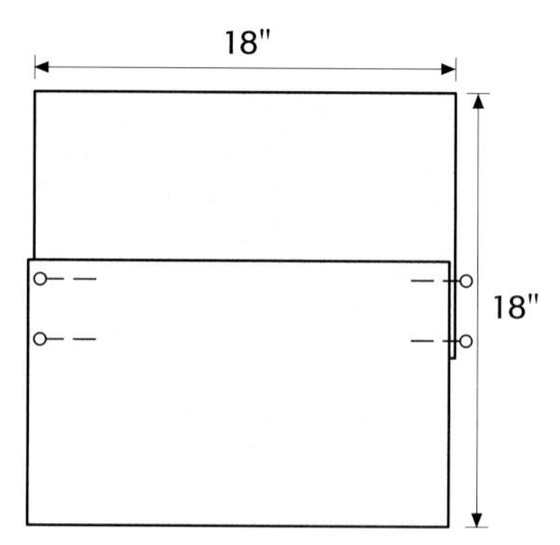

17. Referring to "Cutting and Applying Bias Binding Strips" on pages 39–40, cut 1½"-wide bias strips from the dark-color cotton. Join the strips end to end to make an 80"-long strip.
18. Fold the bias strip around the cotton cording, wrong sides together. Stitch right next to the cording, using a piping or zipper foot on your sewing machine. Trim the seam allowance to ¼".

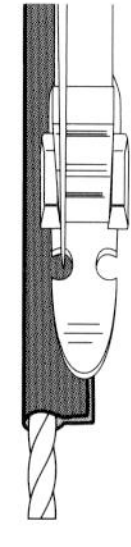

19. Pin the piping to the right side of the pillow top, matching raw edges. Overlap the ends as shown. Clip the piping seam allowances as needed to turn corners smoothly. Baste the piping in place.

20. With right sides together, pin the lapped pillow back over the chenille top. Using a piping or zigzag foot on your sewing machine, stitch close to the piping through all layers. Trim across the corners and turn to the right side. If necessary, lightly steam the seam edges, being careful not to flatten your chenille. Insert the pillow form.

Old-Fashioned Chenille Rug

If you want to re-create the look and feel of old-fashioned chenille, you'll love this chenille rug. By using strips of chenille instead of large sections, you can create chenille designs on solid bases. Dig through old trunks or visit your nearby thrift shops to find authentic vintage chenille designs to duplicate with this fun technique.

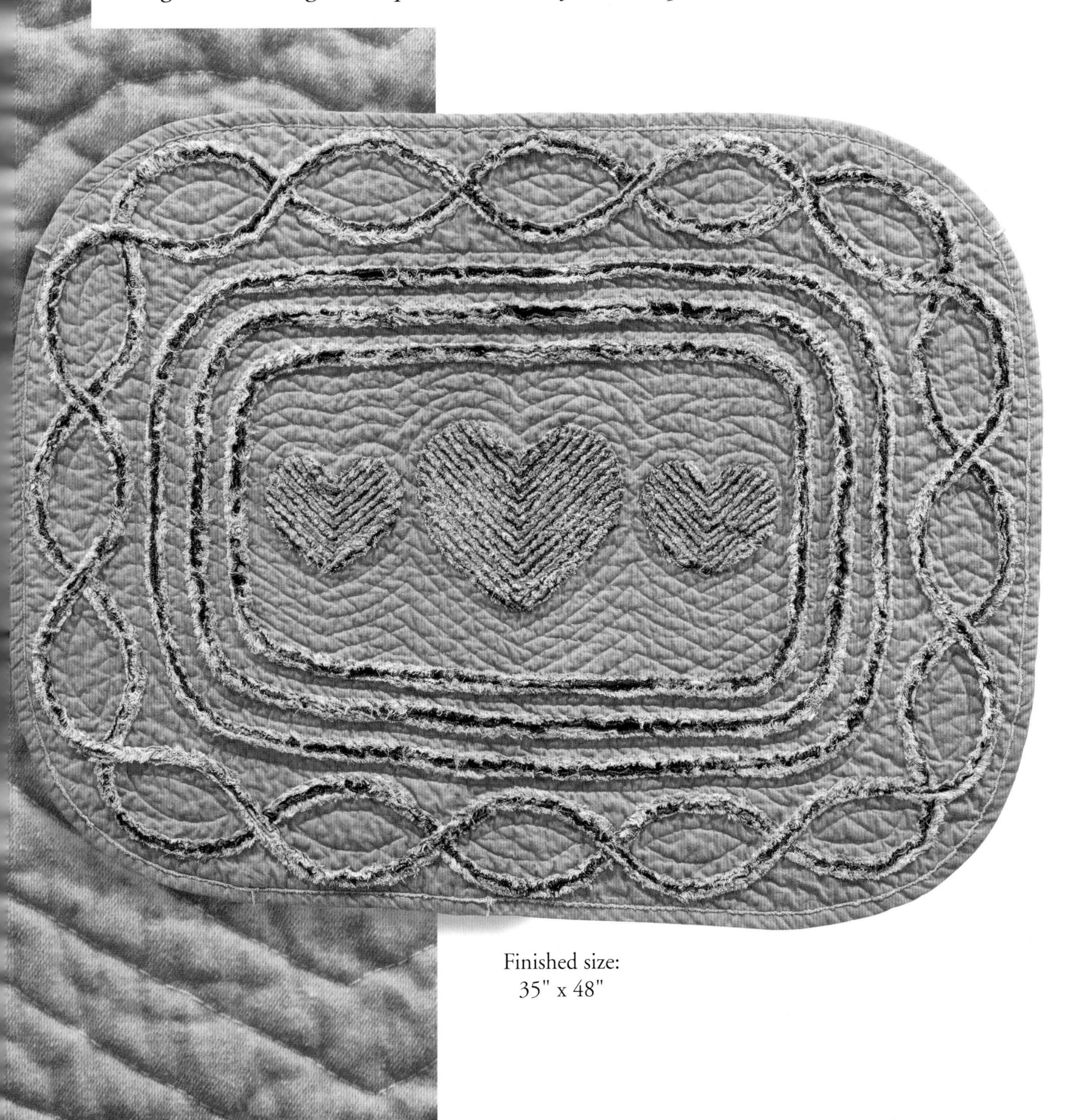

Finished size:
35" x 48"

Yardage Requirements

44"-wide, 100% cotton, unless otherwise specified

2 yds. denim for rug top and binding
1⅜ yds. muslin for rug backing
2¾ yds. needlepunched cotton batting
1 yd. *each* of 5 pieces of 60"-wide, 100% rayon for chenille

Supplies

Coordinating thread
Tailor's chalk
Water-soluble marking pen

Note: 100% rayon will give you the look of old-fashioned, soft chenille. You may substitute cotton but you will need to use an extra layer of needlepunched cotton batting for the base of your chenille stack. The cotton will not fluff enough in the wide border design unless you use the batting to push the layers up. Remember that you may dye the cotton batting to give your chenille stack additional color.

Be sure to make sample blocks of your chenille stack, washing and drying them to make sure your chenille strips will have the coloration and look that you want.

Assembly

1. Referring to "Sample Blocks" on pages 34–35, make sample blocks from the chenille and base fabrics.

2. Cut a 35" x 48" rectangle each from the denim and muslin. Cut 2 rectangles, each 35" x 48", from the batting. Place the muslin rectangle right side down on a flat surface. Layer it with the 2 batting rectangles. Place the denim rectangle, right side up, over the batting.

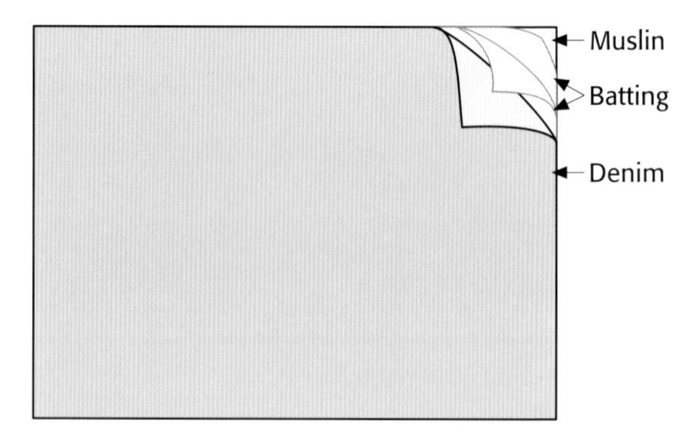

3. Round each corner by placing a dinner plate at the edges and tracing around it. Trim along the drawn lines.

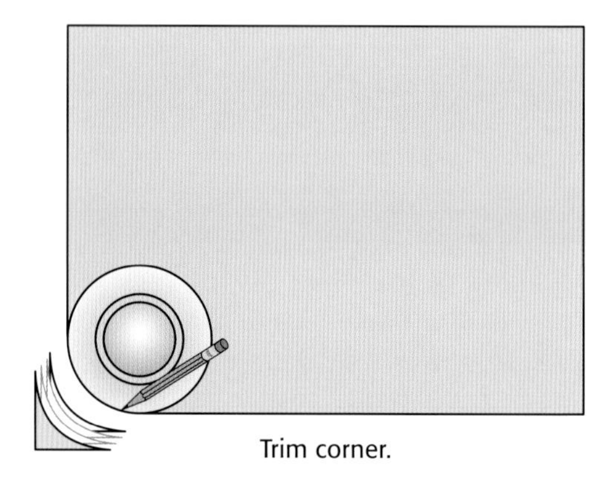

Trim corner.

4. Baste the edges of the rug together. Using a long, diagonal stitch, baste the entire surface of the rug to hold everything in place while you place your chenille design.

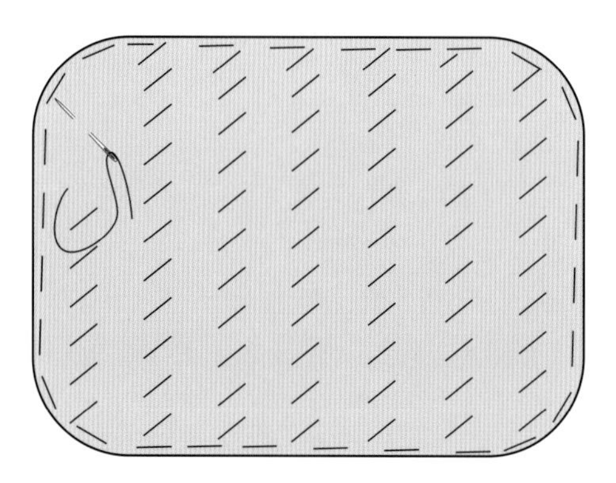

5. Using the marking pen, draw scalloped and inside lines on the rug as shown. Cut a template of the scallop to use as a repeat around the outside edge of the rug.

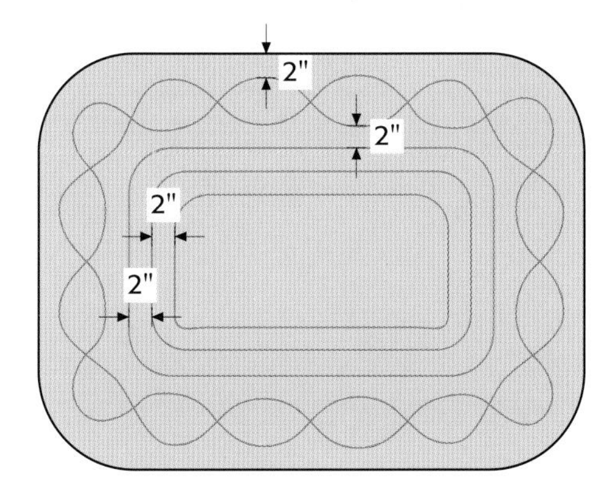

6. Layer the chenille fabrics on a large cutting table, in the same order, bottom to top, as the sample block you selected. Position the ruler at a 45° angle from the right selvage edge. Beginning at the lower right corner, chalk-mark a line to the fabric upper edge. Continue drawing lines 1¼" apart to the left of the first line. You will need approximately 12 to 14 strips to make the rug. Set the unmarked corner aside for the heart templates.

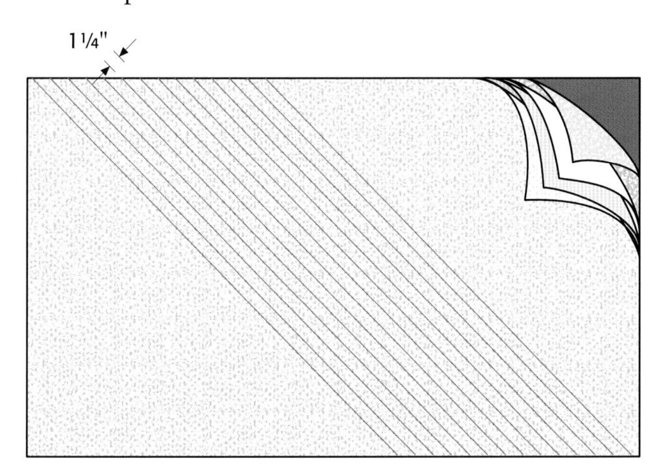

7. Hand baste through the center of the area between the lines to hold the strips together after cutting.

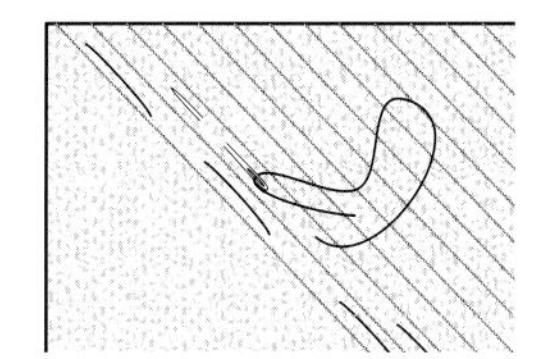

8. Cut the strips apart along the marked lines, using scissors or a rotary cutter and straight-edge ruler. Make a perpendicular cut across the ends of each strip.

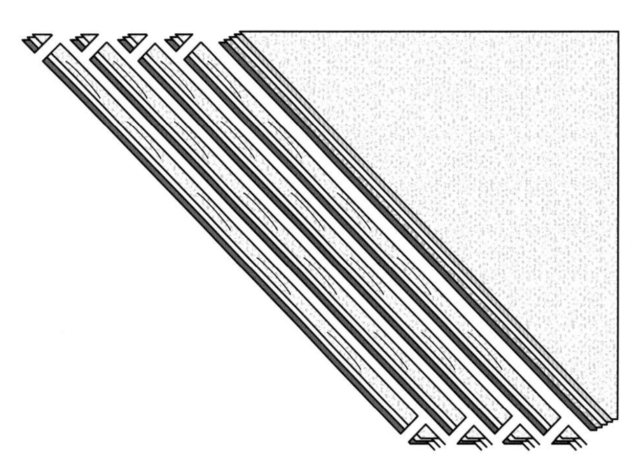

9. Center a strip along one of the scallop lines on the rug. Pin it into place. Continue pinning strips to the line, overlapping the ends by ¼". Overlap the ends ¼" when the strips meet and the line is complete. Stitch down the center of the strip, through all of the layers.

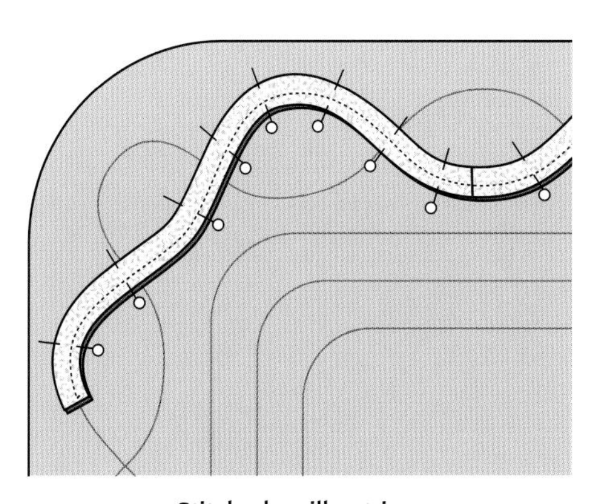

Stitch chenille strip.

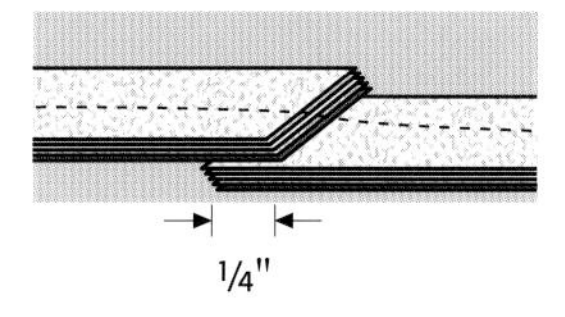

10. Pin and stitch the second row in place in the same manner, crossing over the top of the first row where the two rows intersect.

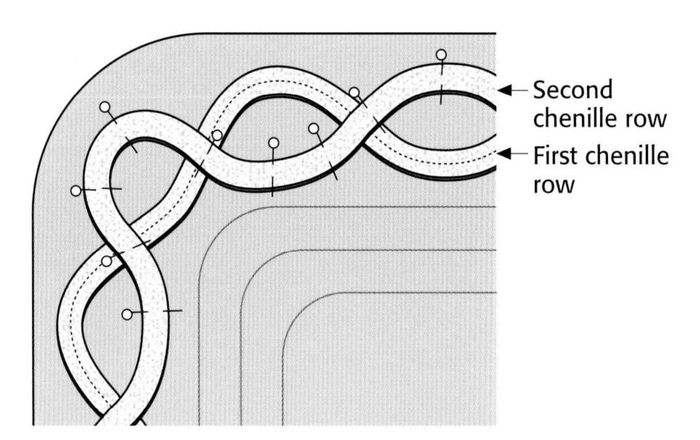

11. Place strips on the 3 inner lines, centering the strips over the lines and lapping ends to make continuous lines as you did for the scallop design. Pin the strips into place and stitch down the center of all the strips; secure with a backstitch at the end.

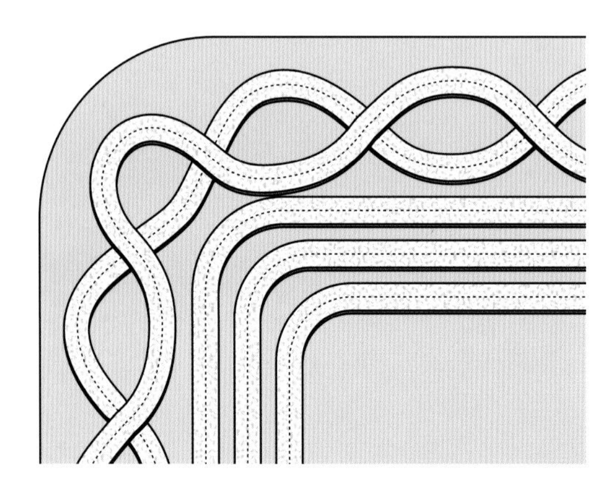

12. Using the patterns on page 95, cut the heart appliqués from the uncut corner of the layered chenille fabrics. Pin the hearts at the edges and centers.

13. Pin the large heart to the rug center. Pin a small heart at each side of the large heart.

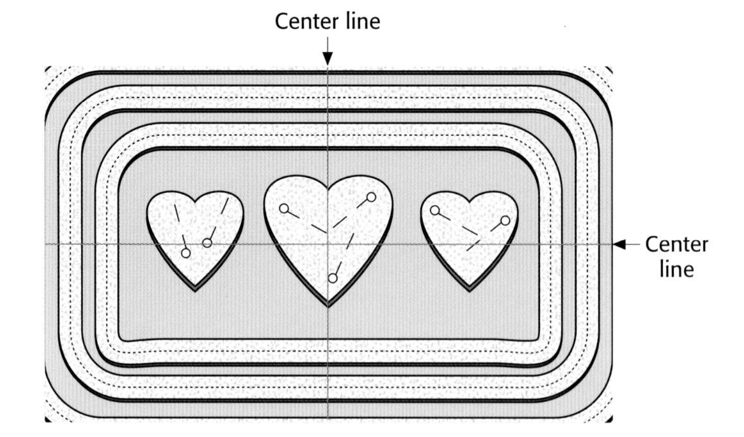

14. Chalk-mark a line down the center of each heart, then mark lines at 45° angles to the center line, forming a V. On each heart, stitch along these lines, then continue stitching parallel rows ⅜" apart until each heart is quilted.

15. Slash the hearts between each row of stitching, cutting all the chenille and appliqué layers (refer to "Sample Blocks" on pages 34–35 for basic cutting directions).
16. Referring to "Cutting and Applying Bias Binding Strips" on pages 39–40, cut enough 1¾"-wide bias strips from the denim to go around the rug perimeter, plus 8". Join the strips end to end.

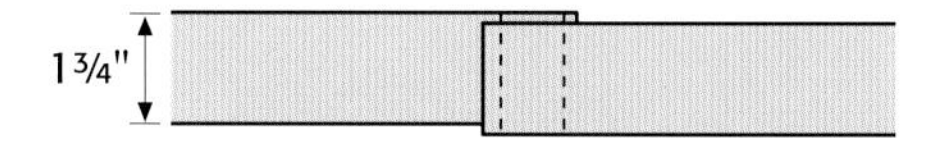

17. On the underside of the rug, chalk-mark a line ¾" from the edge.

18. With right sides together, lay the raw edge of the binding along the chalk line on the rug underside, and pin it in place. Stitch ⅛" from the edge of the binding.

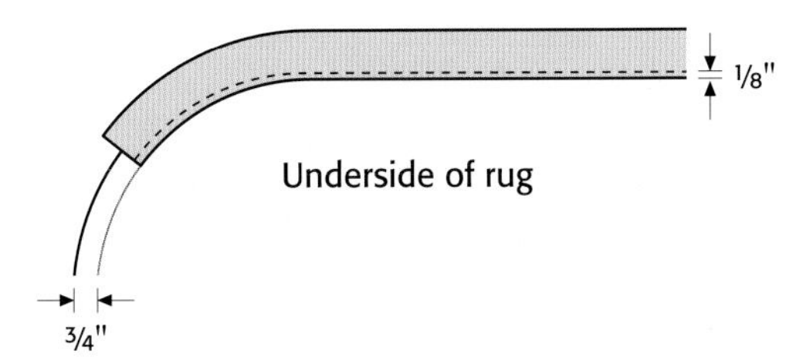

19. On the top of the rug, chalk-mark a line ¾" from the edge. Roll the binding to the top of the rug and pin the edge along the marked line. Stitch ⅛" from the edge.

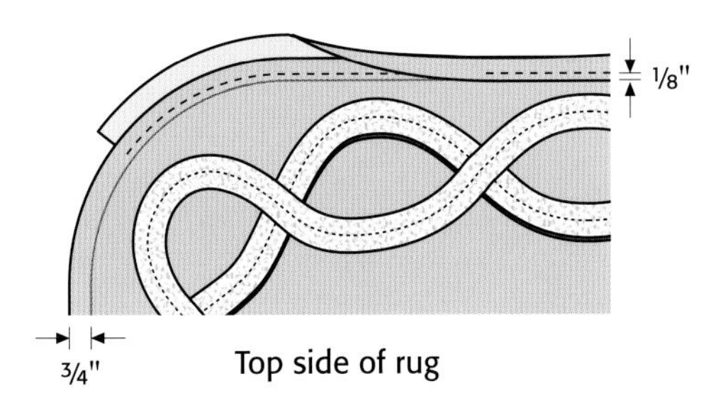

Note: The raw edges of the denim binding will have a soft chenille finish after the rug has been washed and dried. If you use other fabrics for binding, such as 100% cotton, you may wish to bind the rug traditionally, with a finished, turned-under edge.

20. Add decorative quilting to the open areas in the rug. Working from the center section out, echo quilt in 1"-wide rows, following the shapes of the heart designs until the center area is filled. Quilt 1" outside each chenille row. Finally, quilt 1" inside each scallop, making a pointed oval inside each.

21. Wash and dry the rug. Make sure the rug is completely dry before removing it from the dryer. Don't be afraid to give the chenille a "haircut" if some areas are fuzzier than others. With scissors, trim the chenille edges at an angle to give them a smooth soft finish. Take care not to cut deeply into the chenille or it will lose its soft, layered effect.

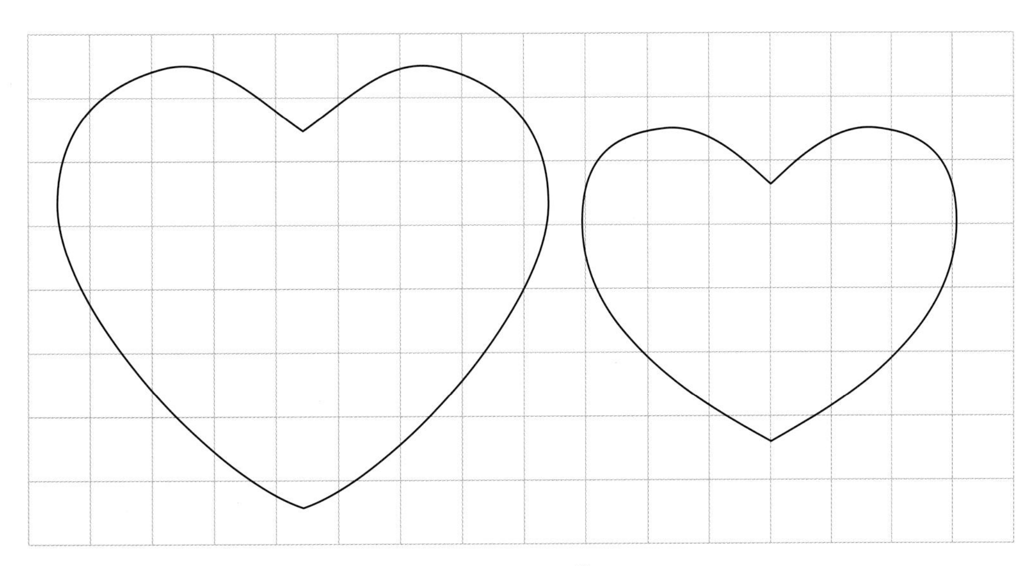

1 square = 1"

Basket Full of Flowers Quilt

Once you discover the texture and elegant look of a chenille quilt, you will want to make more than one. Chenille can take your design to another level, with added depth and a soft, warm feel. Learning how a traditional quilt pattern translates into chenille is a process I find exciting and rewarding. Using one of my favorite quilting designs, I gave this full-size quilt a pieced look without all of the intricate seaming that is part of the traditional block. Stitching the small quilting rows may seem laborious, but because the piecing time is greatly reduced, you will find the total time needed to make the quilt is less than you might think. Discover the possibilities as you begin to quilt in chenille!

Finished size: 90" x 120"

Yardage Requirements

44"-wide, 100% cotton unless otherwise specified

17 yds. of *90"-wide* muslin for chenille layers
4 yds. of light blue for alternate squares
¾ yd. of red for appliqués
1 yd. of purple for appliqués
2 yds. of deep blue for borders and appliqués
⅝ yd. of moss green for appliqués
90" x 120" piece of needlepunched cotton batting

Supplies

Coordinating threads
Water-soluble fabric marker
Water-soluble spray adhesive
Tracing paper
Black felt-tip pen

Cutting

Note: Follow the instructions on page 41 to enlarge the appliqué templates on pages 101–2. When cutting appliqué pieces, take care to cut and place them according to the grain line marked on the pattern.

From the muslin, cut the following pieces:
- 2 rectangles, each 90" x 120"
- 2 rectangles, each 87" x 117"
- 2 strips, each 6" x 117"
- 2 strips, each 6" x 87"
- 17 squares, each 15" x 15"

From the light blue, cut the following pieces:
- 18 squares, each 15" x 15"

From the deep blue, cut the following pieces:
- 2 strips, each 3" x 113"
- 2 strips, each 3" x 83"
- 51 squares, each 2¾" x 2¾"; cut each square in half twice diagonally to make 204 triangles

From the red, cut the following pieces:
- 35 center flowers
- 18 side flowers
- 18 side flowers reversed

From the moss green, cut the following pieces:
- 17 leaves
- 17 leaves reversed
- 36 leaf #1
- 18 leaf #2
- 18 leaf #2 reversed
- 18 stems

From the purple, cut the following pieces:
- 17 handles
- 17 handles reversed
- 17 small hearts
- 18 large hearts

Assembly

1. Make a paper pattern of the Basket and Hearts-and-Flowers blocks, outlining the placement of each appliqué with a black felt-tip pen. Let the ink dry completely.
2. Place a 15" x 15" muslin square over the traced Basket pattern. (Use a light box for positioning if you can't see the design through the muslin square.)
3. Spray adhesive on the backs of the appliqué pieces and press each piece into place on the square, taking care to align the grain line of the appliqués with the grain line of each square. Repeat with the remaining muslin squares.
4. Repeat step 3 with the 15" x 15" light blue squares and the Hearts-and-Flower traced square.

5. On a large, flat surface, place one of the 90" x 120" muslin rectangles. Place the batting rectangle over the muslin, then layer the second 90" x 120" muslin rectangle over it.

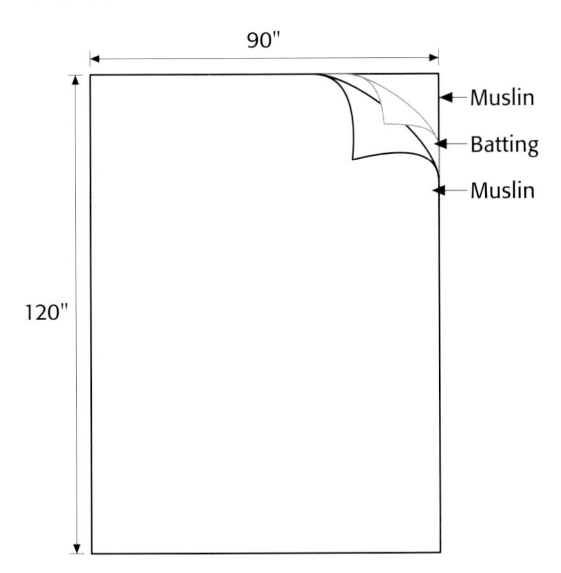

6. Layer both of the 87" x 117" muslin layers on top of the stack, leaving 1½" of the base layers extending beyond the edges.
7. Apply spray adhesive to the 6"-wide muslin strips. Leaving the base layer edges exposed, place the strips around the edge of the chenille layers. Position the side borders first, then the top and bottom borders, overlapping ends at the corners. With the water-soluble fabric marker or pencil, draw a 15"-square grid inside the muslin border.

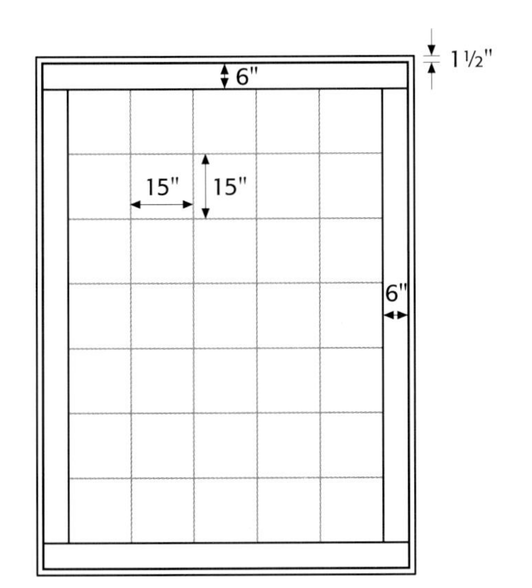

8. Spray the backs of the appliqué squares with spray adhesive. Alternating Basket blocks with Hearts-and-Flower blocks, place the blocks on the chenille base, following the marked grid.

9. Place the dark blue border strips along the inside edge of the 6"-wide muslin border, using the spray adhesive to hold them in place. Carefully overlap edges at the corners so gaps won't open when you stitch.

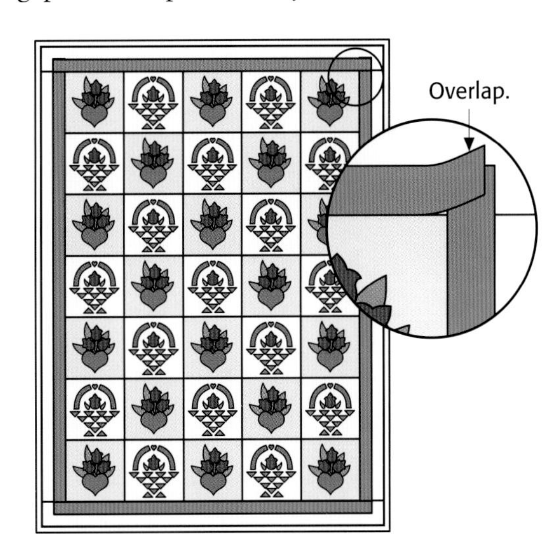

10. Pin block corners, border strips, and appliqué pieces for additional security.

Tip: A tacking gun may be used here if you don't mind sewing over the plastic tabs and having to pull them out later. They don't hold the layers quite as tightly as pins, but they do not fall out or prick your hands as you stitch. Try both methods to find your preference.

11. Draw a 45° angle across the approximate center of the quilt. Stitch along this line, then continue stitching parallel rows ⅜" apart until the quilt is completely stitched.

Note: Once you have stitched the first row, roll one end of your quilt to within a few inches of the stitching line and use large safety pins to pin the rolled edge to the base. It will not open while you stitch the other half. Rolling helps control the large quilt as it goes through your machine. Working with the rolled quilt on your shoulder as you feed it through the machine is also helpful.

12. Slash between each row of stitching, leaving the 3 bottom layers intact (refer to "Sample Blocks" on pages 34–35 for basic cutting directions).
13. Square up the quilt, using a 6" x 24" or 15" x 15" clear plastic cutting guide and rotary cutter, trimming the quilt to the edges of the chenille layers. You will find some distortion and stretching has occurred during the quilting. Try to keep the muslin border the same width on all sides of the quilt. If you find the quilt has distorted more on one edge than another and you must trim the muslin border to 2" wide, adjust the other sides to the same width.
14. Referring to "Cutting and Applying Bias Binding Strips" on pages 39–40, bind the quilt edges with the muslin bias strips.
15. Wash the quilt. You may find it necessary to take the quilt to a commercial Laundromat where you have access to a larger washer and dryer. Set the dryer at "permanent press" and dry completely.

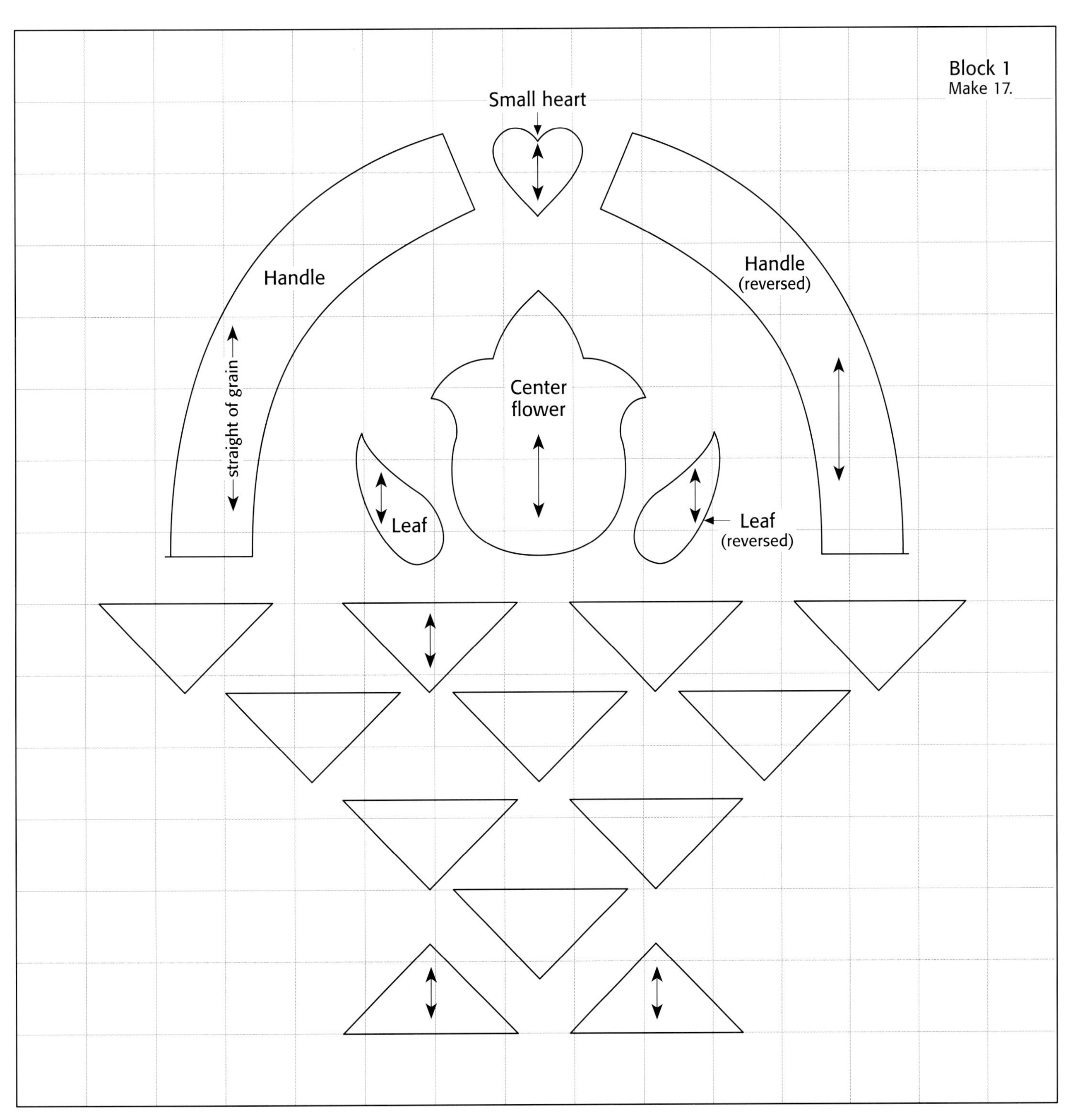
Block 1
Make 17.
Small heart
Handle
Handle
(reversed)
straight of grain
Center
flower
Leaf
Leaf
(reversed)

1 square = 1"

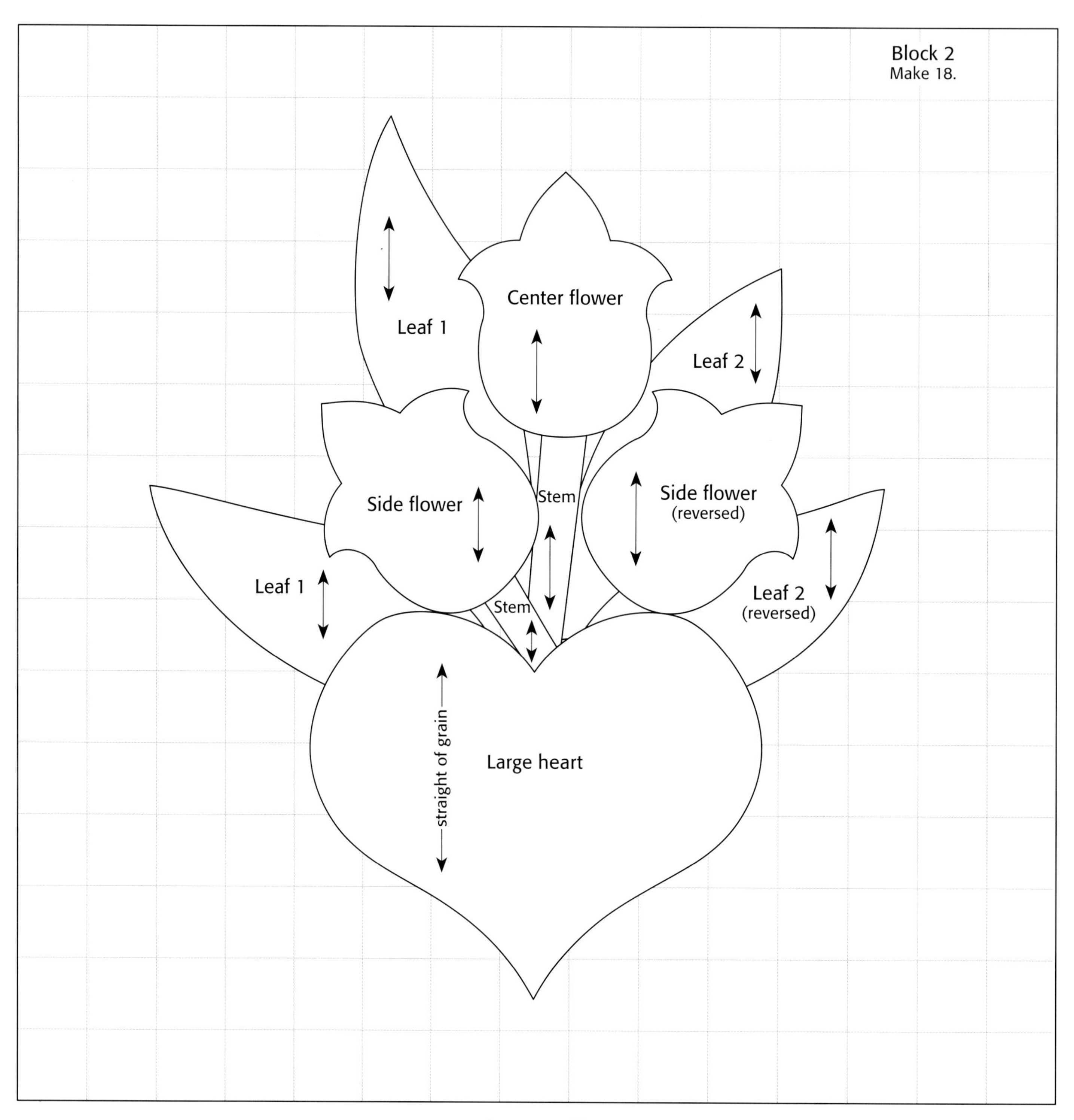
Block 2
Make 18.
Leaf 1
Center flower
Leaf 2
Side flower
Stem
Side flower
(reversed)
Leaf 1
Stem
Leaf 2
(reversed)
straight of grain
Large heart

1 square = 1"

Chenille Bunny

What could be more cuddly than a soft, plush chenille bunny? Chenille appeals to children because of its softness, and to the home decorator because of its color and luxurious visual texture. Whether you're making this charming companion for a special someone or for yourself, you'll love the results.

Yardage Requirements

44"-wide, 100% cotton

5 pieces, each 23" x 58", for chenille layers
1 piece, 25" x 60" for base layer
1 square, 10" x 12", of contrasting fabric for ear lining and nose (suede cloth works well)

Supplies

2 buttons for eyes*
Coordinating thread
Quilting thread
Doll needle
1 yd. ribbon
Large bag of polyester fiberfill for stuffing

*If making bunny for a small child, use childproof eyes and fasten them to the bunny before washing.

Cutting

1. Referring to "Sample Blocks" on pages 34–35, make sample blocks from the chenille and base fabrics.
2. Lay the base layer on a flat surface, right side up. Layer the 5 smaller pieces on top of the base in the same order as your sample block. Leave 1" of base fabric showing around the edges of the top layers. Pin the edges together and place pins randomly over the surface.
3. Chalk-mark a 45° angle across the center of the layered fabric. Stitch the first row of stitching on this line. Continue stitching in parallel rows ½" apart until the fabric is completely quilted.

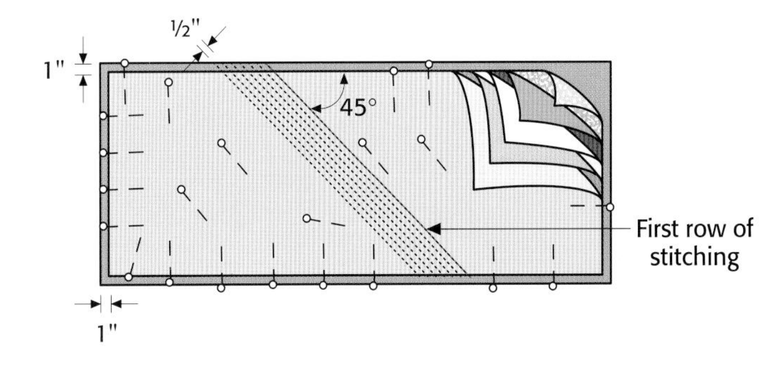

4. Prepare the pattern pieces as described on page 41. Place the pattern pieces (except inner ears and nose) on the fabric according to the pattern layout on page 00 and cut out the pieces.

   Note: Layout is critical. The red lines and arrows on the pattern pieces are not grain lines, they correspond to the chenille stitching lines. It is important to align your chenille lines with the lines on the pattern.

5. Cut out the ear lining and nose, making sure you reverse the pattern pieces to make a right and left ear.

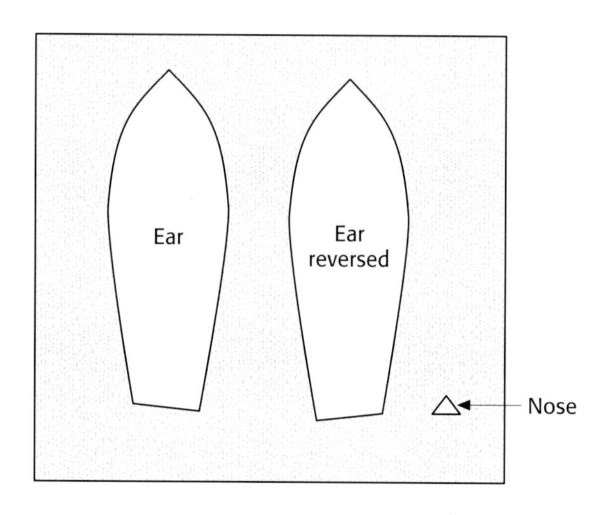

Assembly

Note: Seam allowances are ⅝" wide unless otherwise noted.

Head

1. With right sides together, stitch the center-front head seam. Stitch the nose in place just above the seam allowance on the head right side.

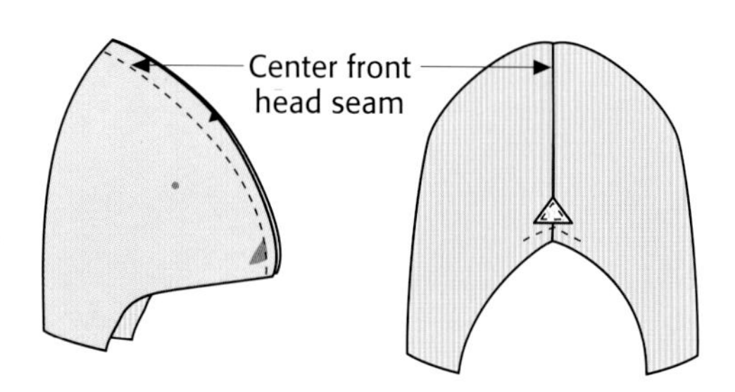

2. Stitch the bunny's lower front head to the front head, matching the center front seam and notch.

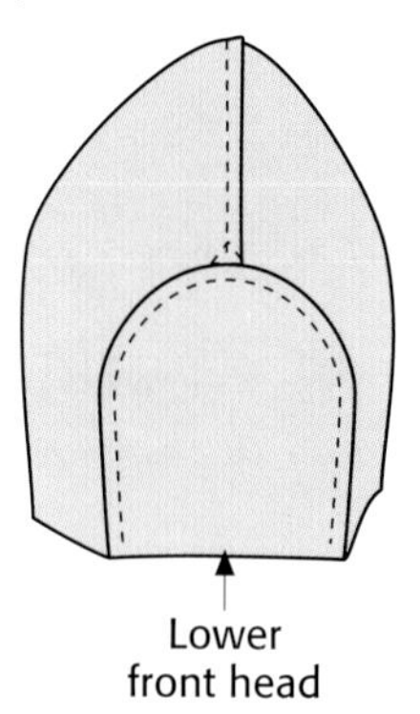

3. Stitch the center-back head seam from point to notches only.

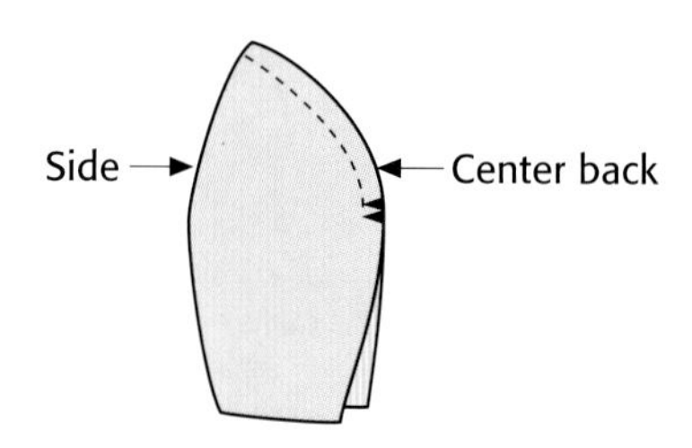

4. Sew the front head to the back head at the side seams.

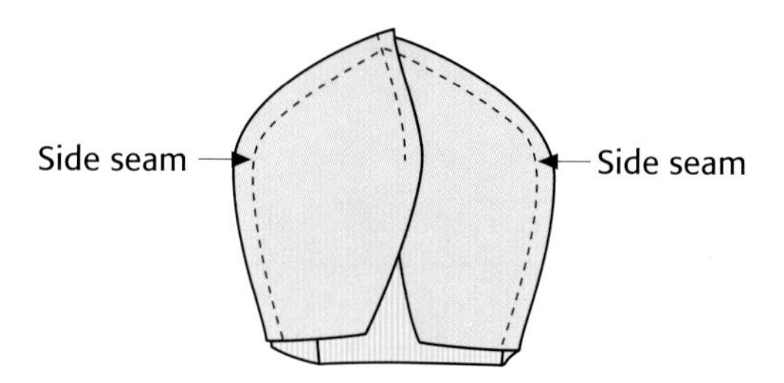

5. With right sides together, sew the ear lining to the ears. Turn to the right side and baste the bottom edges together.

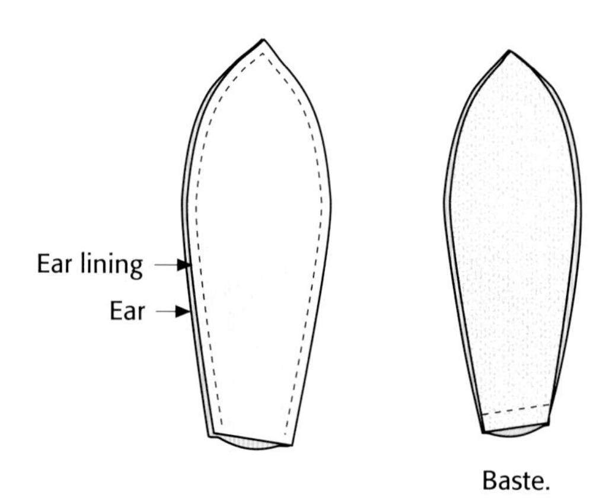

Note: The lining is slightly smaller than the outer ear. Take care to pin the edges together first; the outer ear will have a little extra fullness.

6. Stitch the ears to the head, with the ears centered 1¼" apart across the seam lines at the top of the head as shown. Stitch, trim the seam allowance to ⅛", and zigzag close to the raw edge.

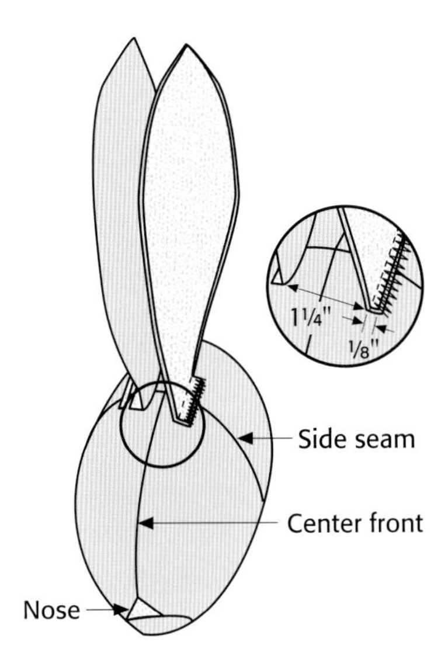

7. Stitch the remainder of the bunny's back head seam.

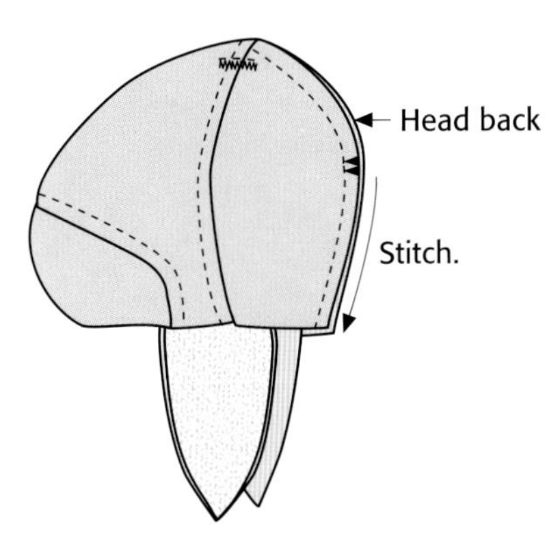

Body

1. Staystitch through all the dots on the back section by stitching along the seam allowance ½" before the dot and ending ½" after the dot, turning corners where necessary. Clip to the stitching, being careful not to cut threads. Stitching from the base-layer side of the piece will be easier than stitching on the chenille side.

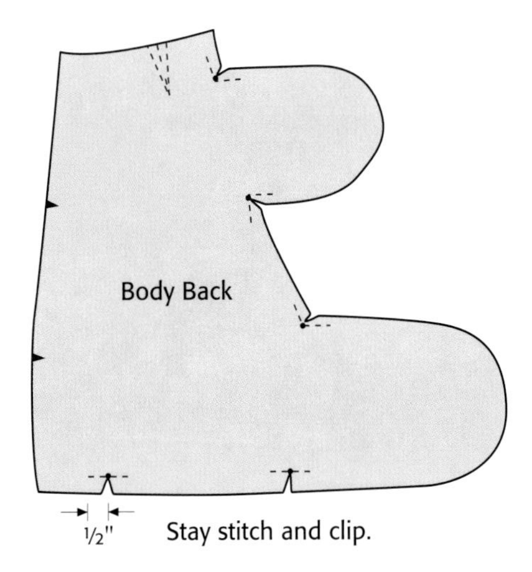

2. Stitch the center-back seam, leaving the area open between the notches.

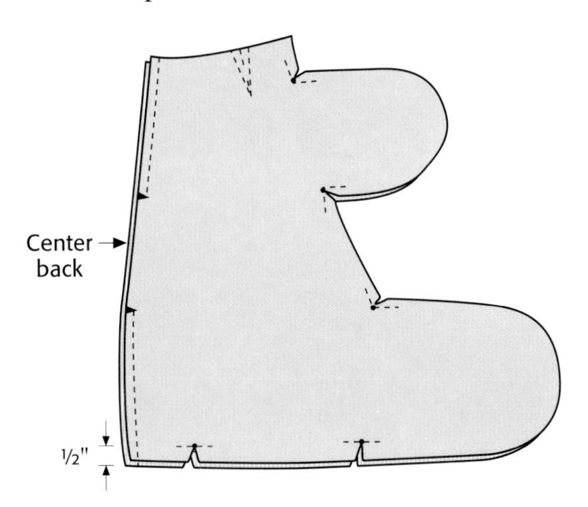

3. Stitch small darts in the neck edge.

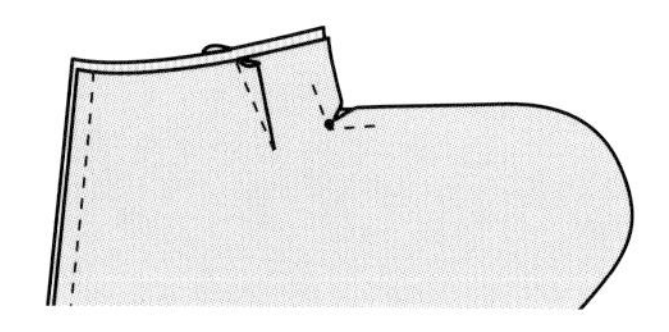

4. Stitch the arm and leg pieces to the bunny body, ending the stitching at the dots.

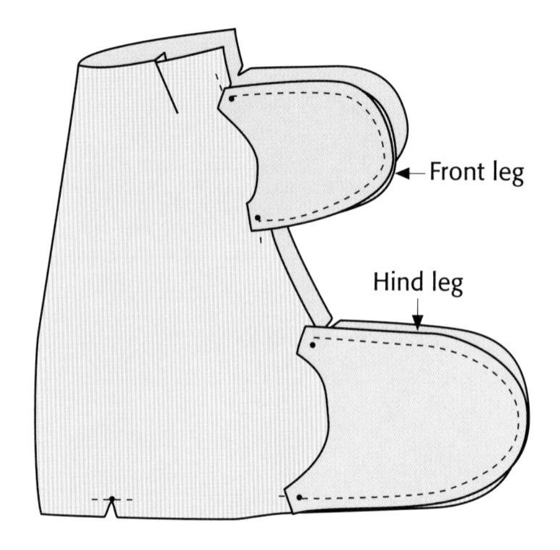

5. Sew the center-front seam.

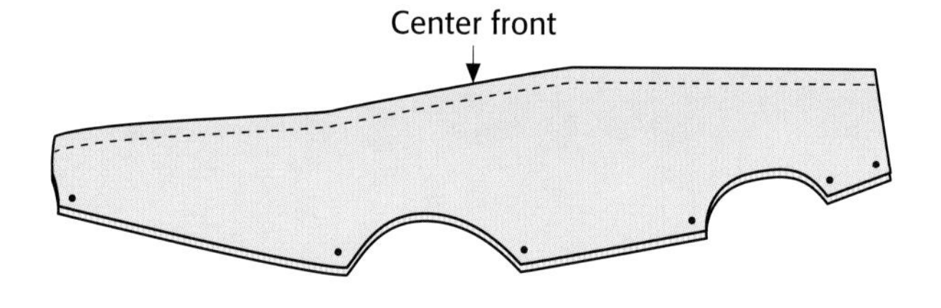

6. Stitch the bunny's front body to the back body, beginning at the neck edge. Stitch the neck seam, ending at the first dot at the upper arm.

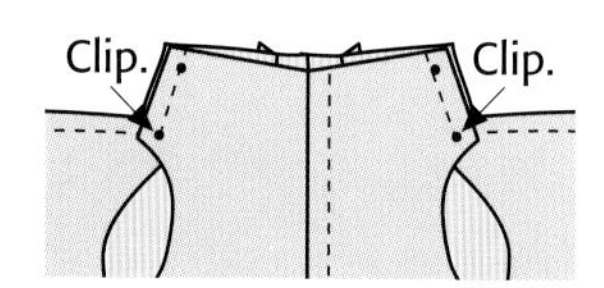

7. Stitch the circular seam joining the bunny arm to the front panel at the next dot.

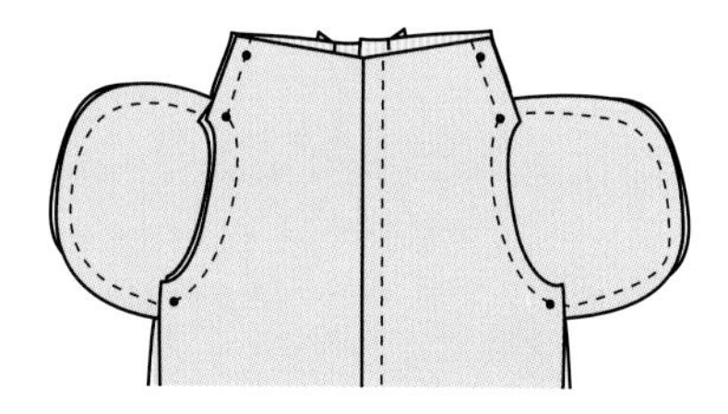

8. Stitch the side straight edge to the next dot.

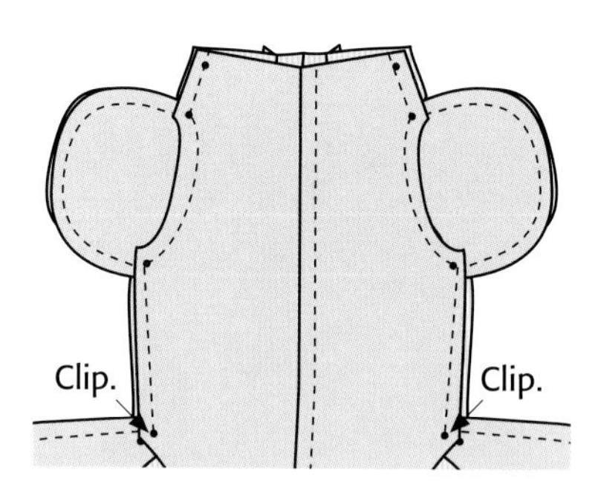

9. Stitch the circular section to the leg section, ending at the next dot at the bottom of the leg. Repeat for the other side.

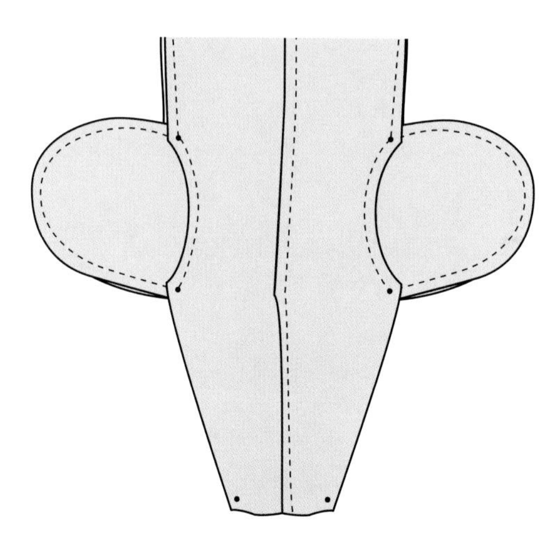

10. With right sides together, sew the tail pieces together with a ¼"-wide seam allowance. Turn and baste the raw edges together.

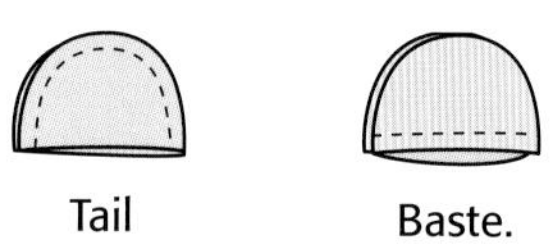

11. Place the raw edge of the tail between the notches on the lower center-back of the bunny body. Baste the tail in place.

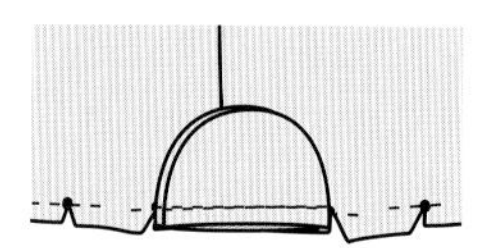

12. Sew the final front body seam to the back body seam from leg to leg, pivoting at the clips at the tail section.

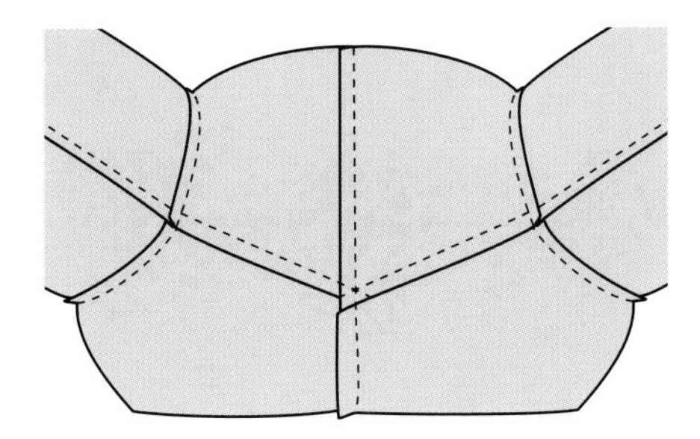

13. Place the head inside the body at the neck edge with right sides together, matching center-front and back seams. The side seams of the head will match the darts in the body. Stitch the head to the body with a ¼"-wide seam allowance. Turn the bunny to the right side.

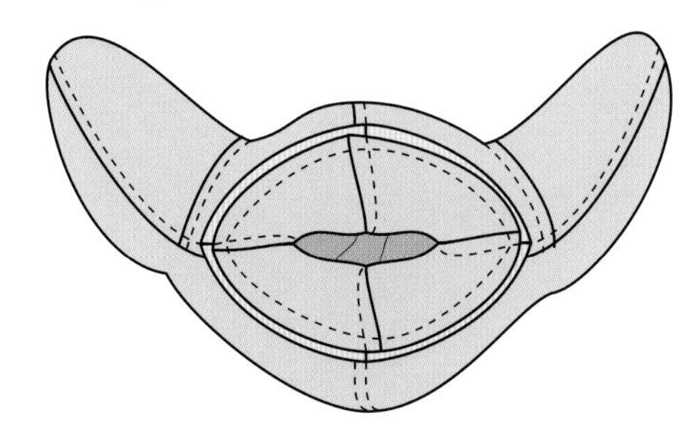

14. Wash and dry the bunny completely.
15. Stuff the bunny and handstitch the center back seam closed.

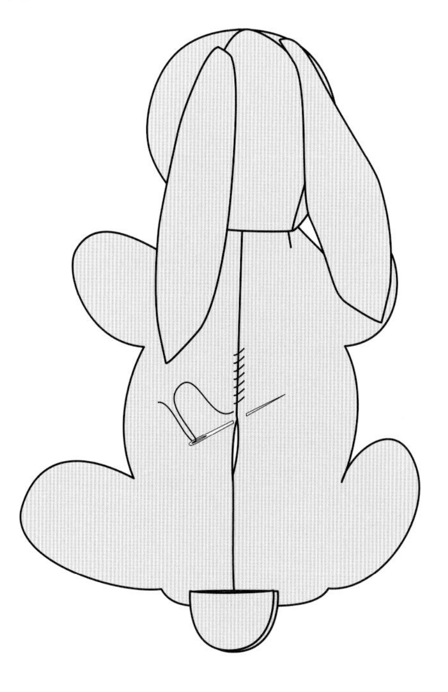

16. Referring to the front head pattern, mark the placement of the eyes and stitch them into place.

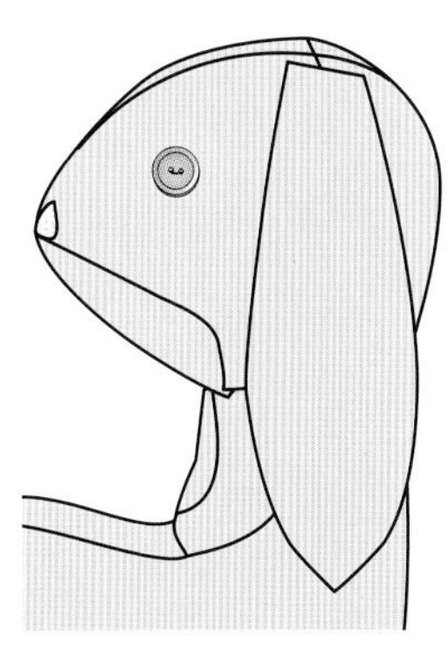

17. With quilting thread and the doll needle, sculpt the face. Begin stitching at the outer edge of the left eye. Secure the thread in place and run the needle through the head from the left eye to the right eye. Pull tightly on the thread until the bunny's head pulls in. Hold in place with your other hand and secure the thread. Do not cut the thread! Continue stitching by running the thread from the right eye down through the head to the center-front neck area just above the neck seam. Pull the needle out and move it over about ¼" and run the needle back up through the head to the left eye. Pull the thread until the chin pulls up and you have the desired shape. Secure and cut the thread.

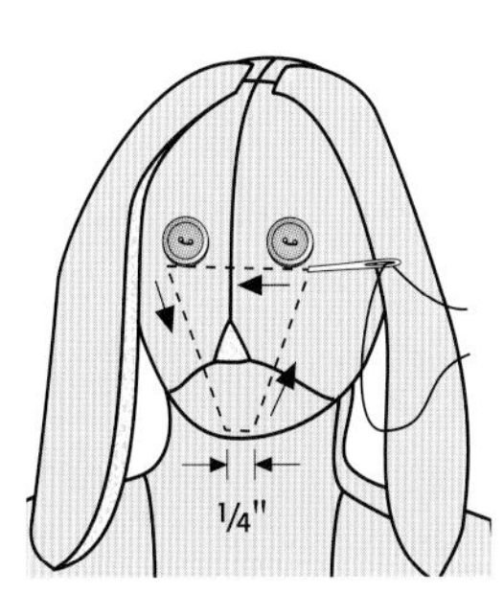

18. Tie a soft ribbon bow around the neck of your cuddly finished bunny!

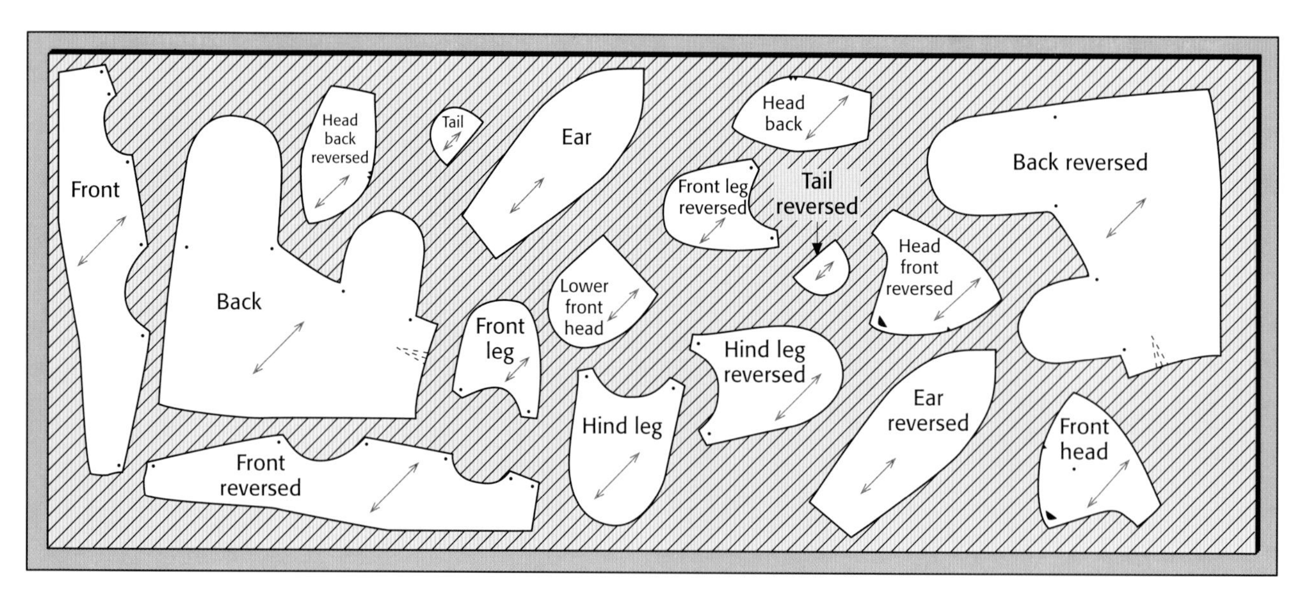

Front
Back
Head back reversed
Tail
Ear
Head back
Back reversed
Front leg reversed
Tail reversed
Head front reversed
Lower front head
Front leg
Hind leg reversed
Hind leg
Ear reversed
Front head
Front reversed

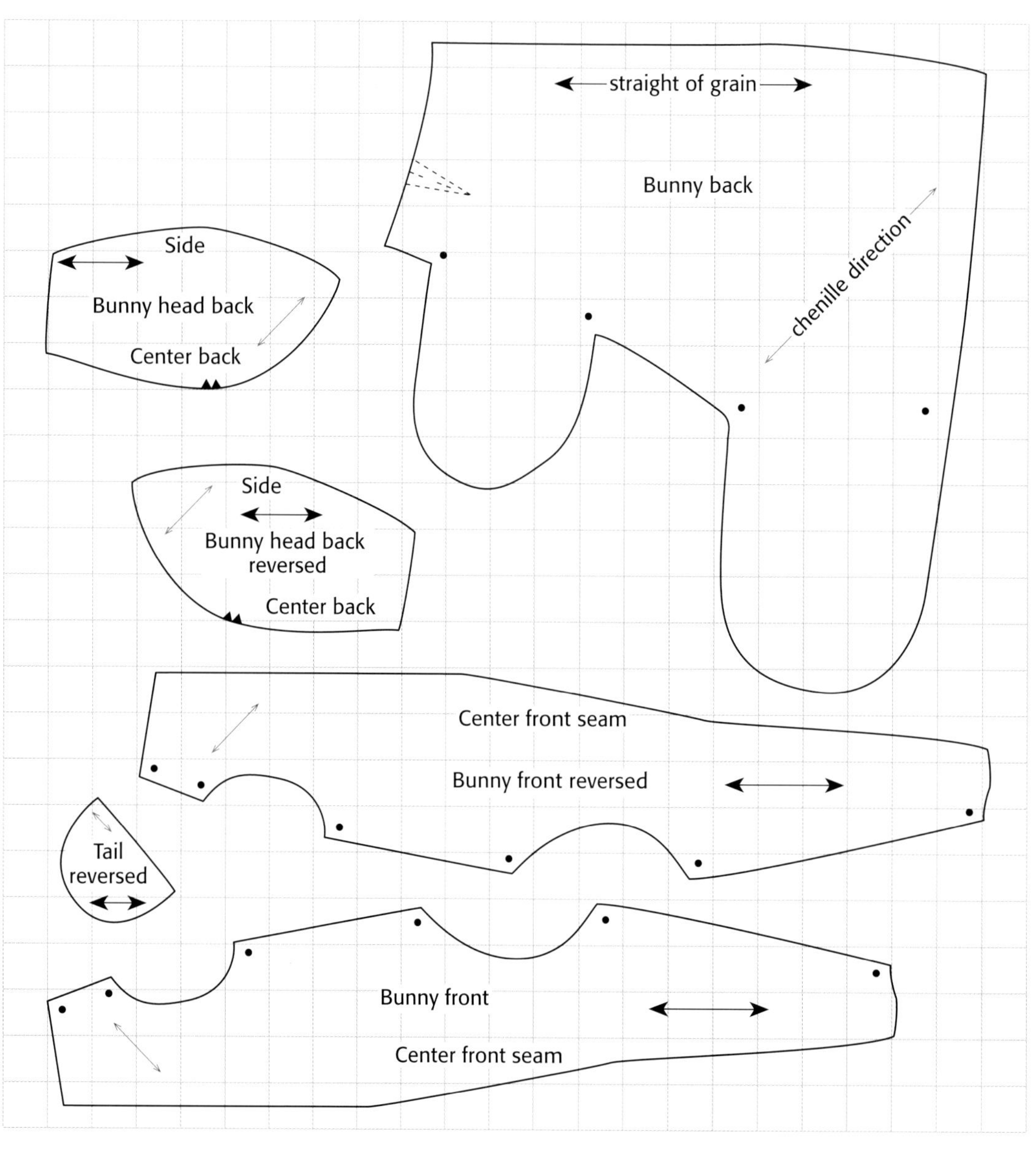

straight of grain
Bunny back
chenille direction
Side
Bunny head back
Center back
Side
Bunny head back reversed
Center back
Center front seam
Bunny front reversed
Tail reversed
Bunny front
Center front seam

1 square = 1"

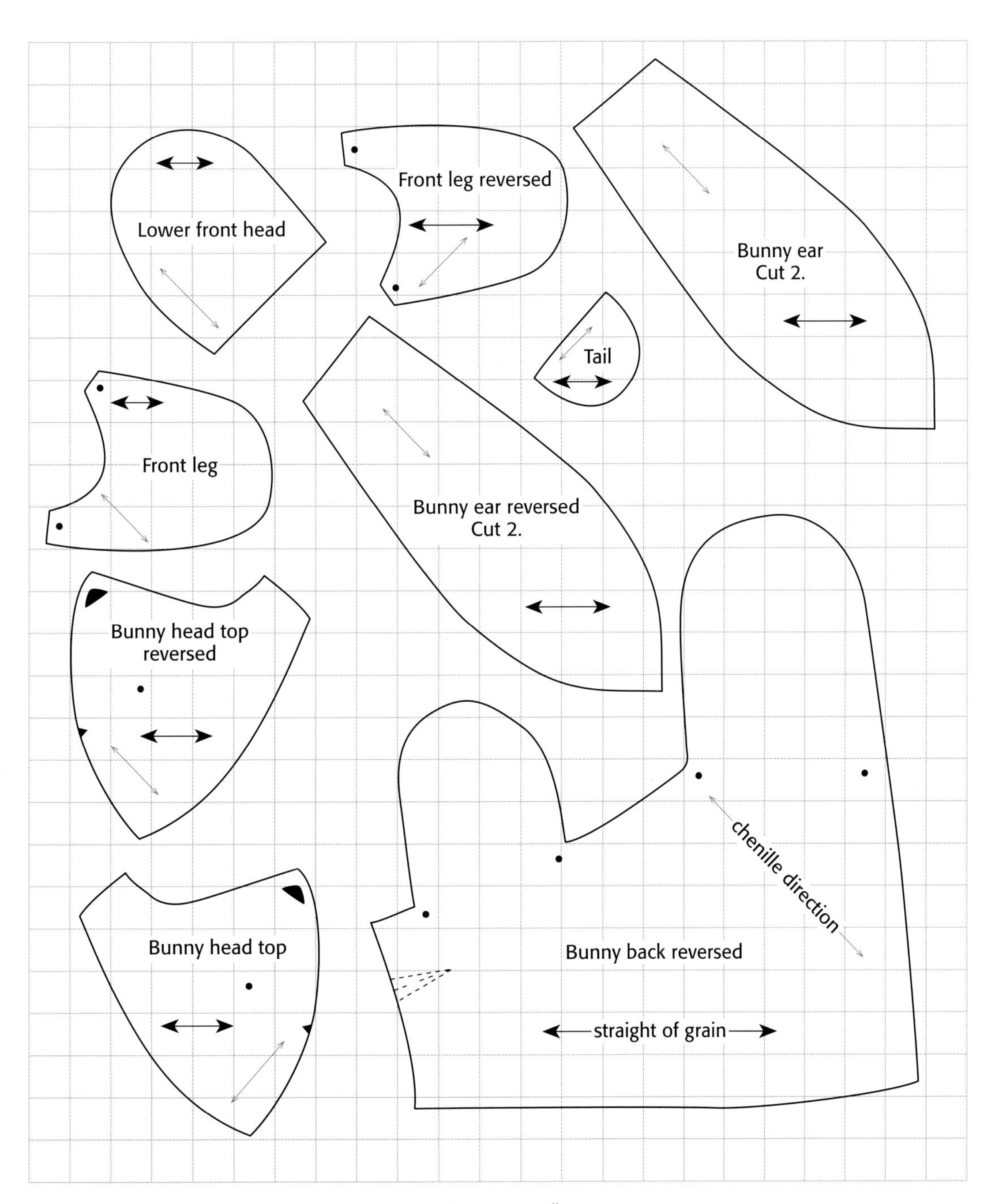
Lower front head
Front leg reversed
Bunny ear
Cut 2.
Tail
Front leg
Bunny ear reversed
Cut 2.
Bunny head top
reversed
Bunny head top
chenille direction
Bunny back reversed
straight of grain

1 square = 1"

About the Author

Nannette Barlow Holmberg studied fashion design at Utah State University and the Fashion Institute of Technology in New York City before opening her first store in Utah in 1970. For more than twenty-five years, she has designed fashions in her stores.

Nannette began creating wearable art in 1985. Since then, her work has been shown and sold in museums, galleries, and boutiques throughout the West. Her passion led her to develop a fashion-design program for the Utah State Board of Education. In addition to teaching workshops thoughout the country, Nannette is a designer for McCall's Pattern Company. She is currently working on a complete line of clothing and travels all over the world looking for resources. Her love of design and wearable art has made it possible for her fondest dreams to come true.

Nannette lives in Salt Lake City, Utah, with her husband, David, and her daughter, Erin.